# Civil Wars: From Dublin to South Russia and Return Journey

Clare Scott

&

William Gerald Forbes Scott

www.southrussiadiary.wordpress.com

For my Mam & Dad

For Granddad & Granny


In remembrance of my uncle

James (Jim) MacNamara

d. May 2021

# Contents

*Image List* ...................................................................... v

*Preface* ........................................................................... xi

**Chapter One: Beginnings** ............................................. 3

   *Loch Lomond to Glasgow* ........................................ 5

   *Dublin* ........................................................................ 6

   *Signing up* ................................................................. 8

   *Churchill & the Bolsheviks* ...................................... 9

   *Rest Camps* ............................................................. 15

**Chapter Two: Here be Monsters** ................................. 21

   *Into the Mediterranean* ......................................... 24

   *Etna & the Messina Disaster* ................................ 27

   *Malta* ....................................................................... 29

   *Lemnos & Moudros* ............................................... 35

**Chapter Three: Constantinople** ................................. 39

   *At the Gates of War* .............................................. 41

   *Constantinople* ...................................................... 42

   *St. Sophie* ............................................................... 44

   *A Day Out* .............................................................. 50

    *The Mad Dervishes* ............................................................... *52*

**Chapter Four: Into the Black Sea** ............................................**59**

    *Fifteen Sunken Ships* ......................................................... *66*

**Chapter Five: The War in South Russia** ................................**69**

    *A SitRep* ............................................................................. *72*

    *The British in Russia* ......................................................... *73*

    *War Matériel* ..................................................................... *74*

    *The Volunteer Army and The White Army* ....................... *78*

    *The Cossacks* .................................................................... *82*

    *The Dashing General Pytor Wrangel* ................................ *84*

    *The Red Army* ................................................................... *86*

    *The Green Army* ............................................................... *86*

    *The Black and Blue Armies* ............................................... *87*

**Chapter Six: Up the Line** .........................................................**91**

    *Railway War* ...................................................................... *93*

    *Taganrog* ........................................................................... *96*

    *The RAF in South Russia* ................................................... *98*

    *'The Bolshies are steadily advancing'* ............................. *102*

    *Death on the Steppe* ...................................................... *106*

**Chapter Seven: Retreat** .........................................................**113**

  *Leaving Taganrog*......................................................................*115*

  *Last Train Over Rostov Bridge* .......................................................*120*

  *Ekaterodinar*.............................................................................*128*

**Chapter Eight: Novorossiysk** ......................................................... **133**

  *The Green Guards* ....................................................................*136*

  *A Princess & a Marriage*............................................................*145*

  *Duck!* ......................................................................................*149*

  *Frozen*....................................................................................*152*

**Chapter Nine: Evacuation** .............................................................. **157**

  *The British Prepare to Leave* .....................................................*159*

  *Civilians* .................................................................................*166*

  *A Lovely Sight..* .........................................................................*172*

**Chapter Ten: The Journey Home** .................................................... **181**

  *Theodosia*................................................................................*183*

  *The Fez* ...................................................................................*185*

  *Chanak & Kantara* ...................................................................*188*

**Chapter Eleven: Frying Pan to Fire** ................................................. **193**

  *The Irish War of Independence* ..................................................*197*

  *The Treaty* ..............................................................................*202*

  *Civil War once more* ................................................................*203*

*Kerry* .................................................................................... 207

*Guardian of the Peace* ........................................................ 210

*Graiguenamanagh* ............................................................. 212

*Family* .................................................................................. 215

*Mutt & Jeff* ......................................................................... 224

*Acknowledgements* ............................................................ 227

**Appendices** ............................................................................. **230**

*Suggested Reading* ............................................................. 230

*Other Voices* ....................................................................... 233

*The Other Granddad* ......................................................... 236

*The Campile Bombing* ....................................................... 237

*Select Bibliography* ............................................................ 241

*Index* .................................................................................... 245

# Image List

*Fig. 1.* Gerald Scott, Kerry, 1922. Photographer Unknown. Source: Anthony Scott.

*Fig. 2.* Winston Churchill in October 1918. Photographer Unknown. Source: Imperial War Museum.

*Fig. 3.* The *Maid of Orleans*, 1920, from the Roy Thornton Collection. Source: Thornton, Goodfellow, 1913.

*Fig. 4.* Rest Camp No.3 on the Leas in Folkestone. Source: Dover and Folkestone During the Great War, Barnsley: Pen & Sword Military, George, 2008.

*Fig. 5. Porto* as the Prinz Heinrich from Edwin Drechsel in *Norddeutscher Lloyd*, Bremen: 1857-1970, Vol. I Cordillera Publishing Co., Vancouver, 1994.

*Fig. 6.* Street in Messina, Sicily, showing damage caused by the earthquake, January 1909. Collection of Lieutenant Commander Richard Wainwright, 1928.

*Fig. 7. An Armenian,* Scribner's 1893, *Collection of Maggie Land Blanck.* Source: www.maggieblanck.com, 2012.

*Fig. 8. Galata Bridge, Constantinople, December 5th*, 1919. Photo George Swain. Source: *The Documentary Imagination (Part Two), A Day's Journey: Constantinople December 9th 1919*, in *The Michigan Quarterly Review*, Vol. XLV, Issue 1, Winter 2006.

Fig. 9. *Whirling dervishes in Galata Mawlawi House 1870*. Photo: Pascal Seba.

Fig. 10. Steamer *Huntscastle* loading at Kantara, 1918. Source: National Library of New Zealand, (2017).

Fig. 11. *General Herbert Holman, July 1919*. Photographer Unknown. Source: IWM

Fig. 12. *General Anton Denikin c. 1918*, Photographer: Unknown. Source: *The Times History of the War*. London: The Times, p. 399

Fig. 13. *General Pytor Wrangel in Sevastopol in April 1920*. Photographer Unknown. Source, www.en.topwar.rum 2004.

Fig. 14. *Black Army leader Nestor Makhno in a holding camp for displaced persons in Romania, c. 1921*. Photographer Unknown/Public Domain. Source: Wikipedia.

Fig. 15. *Air Ace, Raymond Collishaw*, Photographer Unknown, Source: Nanaimo Airport, British Columbia.

Fig. 16. *Captain William Frecheville of the Royal Engineers*. Photographer Unknown. Source: *www.ewhurstfallen.co.uk*. 2005.

Fig. 17. *Novorossisk, c. 1906*, Old Postcard. Photographer Unknown.

Fig. 18. *The Benbow underway, January 1917*. Photographer Unknown/Public Domain. Source: IWM.

*Fig. 19. Lieutenant Colonel Bingham.* Image: Lancing College War Memorial. Source: www.hambo.org

*Fig. 20. Novorossisk, March 1920.* Photographer Unknown/Public Domain. Source: Wikipedia.

*Fig. 21. SMS Hannover's* sister ship, *SMS Schlesien.* (North Atlantic Seaway by N.R.P. Bonsor, vol.2, p.561) Gröner, Erich (1990). German Warships: 1815–1945. I: Major Surface Vessels. Annapolis: Naval Institute Press.

*Fig. 22. HMS Czar,* Photographer Unknown/Public Domain. Source: Wikipedia.

*Fig. 23.* Letter from Gerald Scott in the Irish Independent Newspaper 1968. Courtesy Anthony Scott.

*Fig. 24.* Gerald Scott and friends messing around in Kerry, 1922. Photographer Unknown. Source: Anthony Scott. Kerry 1922.

*Fig. 25. Gerald Scott and friends, Kerry, 1922.* Photographer Unknown. Source: Anthony Scott. Kerry 1922

*Fig. 26. With dachshund.* Courtesy Anthony Scott.

*Fig. 27. Gerald Scott, family and colleagues.* Courtesy Anthony Scott.

*Fig. 28. Gerald and Elizabeth*, Baldwinstown. Photo Anthony Scott..

*Fig. 29. Granddad,* Seaview Terrace Co. Wexford, 1970s. Photo by and courtesy Anthony Scott.

*Fig. 30. Gerald Scott's Medals.* Photo by and courtesy of Selina and Joe Scott.

*Fig. 31.* John Mac. Courtesy Kathleen Scott.

**Maps**

Map. 1. Scotland

Map. 2. Europe c.1919

Map. 3. Russia

Map. 4. South Russia around Rostov

Map. 5. South Russia around Rostov

**Maps and illustrations are by the author**

**FIG.1.     GERALD SCOTT, KERRY, 1922. PHOTOGRAPHER UNKNOWN.  SOURCE: ANTHONY SCOTT.**

## Preface

My granddad, William Gerald Forbes Scott (1899-1977), was an apprentice in Dublin when he joined the British army in 1918. He then volunteered or was assigned to the British Military Mission which was mobilized by Churchill to assist the White Army in the war in Russia against the Bolsheviks between 1919 and 1920. His account maps the trip by boat from Wendover to France then down to Marseille by train, across the Mediterranean via Malta and Greece to Istanbul (Constantinople as it was then) and through the Black Sea to Novorossiysk. After a short time up the line at Taganrog, the Mission retreated back to Novorossiysk where it assisted in the disposal of war supplies and the evacuation of soldiers and civilians as the Bolsheviks advanced, before returning to England via Egypt.

I was eleven when he died so I have few memories of him. Having lived abroad for a time, I returned to County Waterford in the new millennia and began to put down roots. I didn't know any of my grandparents well. When I was younger this did not seem of great importance but as the years passed, I became more curious about how I was connected to the world and what my place was in it. I was familiar with my granddad's account of his 'Russian Adventure' for many years, and it had always struck me as being both very short and very dull. This small brown notebook written in longhand after the return from South Russia, rather than telling romantic tales of derring-do on the vast windswept Steppe seemed to contain little more than ship's names, times, and dates of departures. While there are other things mentioned in this tiny notebook - a Russian Princess, a whale, Mount Etna, a marriage, duck hunting on the Black Sea, divers in Malta, sunken ships, Dervishes, Mount Etna, The Hagia Sophia, executions, plague, quarantine, a funeral - his account is tantalizingly sparse with few clues as to how he felt about being part, however small, of momentous events. But, over time I began to catch glimpses of what my grandfather was trying to process in setting down his words in a time when men, or indeed anyone, did not talk of their feelings. Images began to flicker in my mind's eye, Like the flanks of silvery fish flashing in murky water, and I determined to haul what I could to the surface, to uncover the richness that I sensed lay beneath.

*Civil Wars: From Dublin to South Russia and Return Journey* is an effort to contextualise the events, places and people he refers to, fleshing them out with historical detail and personal anecdote. It also touches on events in Ireland from the Lock Out to the Rising to the War of Independence and the Civil War and the subsequent new Free State, reflections of which are found in my granddad's life from losing a brother in the 1916 Rising, witnessing the death of Sean Treacy on a Dublin Street, taking part in the Kerry Landings and later experiences as a member of the Garda Siochana through the Second World War. By weaving his personal account with my own research and family lore into the wider tapestry of history, I hope to create a story that might seem familiar, a history of a life that spanned the bones of a century of turbulence, the eddies of which still crackle in our tangled genetic heritage.

## Notes on the text

*The entirety of the text in the notebook is included here in bold italic. Quotes from other sources are in regular italic. A selection of the handwritten pages from the notebook act as chapter headings though not all of the 48 pages are included.*

*I have kept the spellings in the quotes from the diary as they are, which are for the most part correct. Any seeming errors are in the place names which have changed over time. The most obvious is that granddad spelled Novorossisk with no 'y' which I have retained in places though 'Novorossiysk' is also used. It was also spelled 'Novorossiisk'. For the rest, when they are not direct quotes, they adhere to contemporary spelling.*

*Dates in some sources are confusing not only because the White Army were using the Julian calendar (13 days behind) but because of the sheer number of events too. My granddad's notebook is unusual in that it seems to be precise about dates which he invariably pairs with days of the week and, which all match up, which leads me to think he wrote it directly after his return in 1920.*

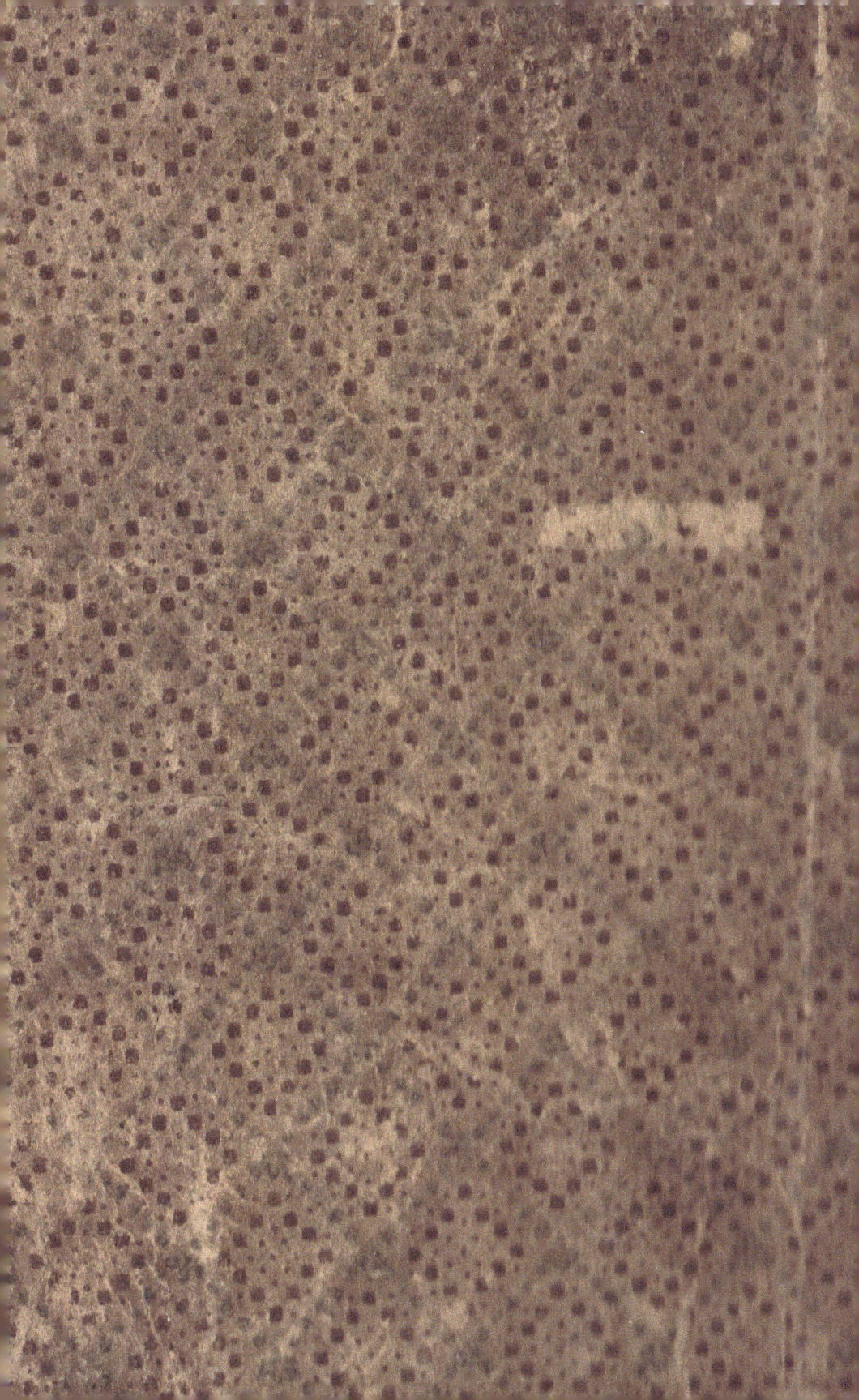

# Diary

...om Buckinghamshir[e]
...ch Russia & Retu[rn]
Journey.

We left Wend[over]
1.30 pm on Thurs[day]
...th Oct. 1919 and ar[rived]
Dover at 8-30 p[m]
...e same date. W[e]
...ent that night [to]
...o. 2 Rest Camp and
...barked at 12 no[on]
Friday 31st Oct 1919

# Chapter One: Beginnings

## Loch Lomond to Glasgow

William and Annie Scott (nee Bryce) had grown up in neighbouring villages, Balloch and Alexandria, on the river Leven which empties from Loch Lomond into the Clyde. Within easy reach of Glasgow, the area around Loch Lomond is beautiful. It straddles the Highland Boundary Fault which is considered the border between the lowlands and highlands of Scotland. It is the sort of landscape that is familiar to an Irish person - the mountains, the sea. We are all familiar with the rush of recognition we get when, returning from a long trip, the shifting line of the horizon locks into its familiar shape. It is hardly a reach to suppose if a family had lived in an area for generations before dispersing, descendants might recognise and gravitate to a similar environment. That is to say that the view from Balloch seemed familiar when I visited in 2018. Discovering the landscape my great-grandparents lived in brought them closer. Sitting in the parkland above Loch Lomond, I wondered if my great-grandparents had perhaps courted there. Mountains and water were never far from the lives of my ancestors and have been elements in all the places that I have lived.

William and Annie moved after their wedding closer to Clydebank where William worked and their son, the subject of this book, William Gerald Forbes Scott, was born on September 3rd, 1899, in the Parish of Old Kilpatrick in the county of Dumbarton. Old

Kilpatrick is a village, now a satellite of Glasgow, on the Clyde. Though he was christened William Gerald Forbes Scott, my granddad's first name in the records is Gerald, probably to distinguish him from his father. It was common practice in Ireland for people to use their second names for everyday use, keeping their first name for occasions, as if somehow it might wear out.

## Dublin

William and Annie moved to Dublin in the year after my grandfather's birth where William was appointed skipper of a bucket ladder dredger on Dublin's Docks. Bucket dredgers were in common use at that time but have been superseded by other forms of dredging. A bucket dredger is stationary, fixed on anchors while an endless chain of buckets fills along a slanting track that scrapes the bottom. The buckets turn upside down and empty as they move over the tumbler at the top to begin their descent once again. The dredged material is then loaded onto barges and taken out to sea to be dumped. By 1911 William was a dredging master in charge of three dredgers and the family were living in East Wall, Dublin, just around the corner from playwright Sean O'Casey and surviving comfortably but these were turbulent times. In 1913 there was the Dublin lock-out, a general strike which lasted seven months and would become a watershed moment in Irish labour history. Though it does not seem to have particularly impacted the Scotts, it cannot have passed unnoticed. It caused hardship to thousands in the city and eventually many workers were forced to leave the unions to avoid starvation while black-listed workers had little choice but to join the British Army to fight, and perhaps die, in the Great War. Worker's revolutions had more success elsewhere, as young Gerald would see.

**Two Tragedies**

War would come to Dublin before long with the Easter Rebellion but before that, tragedy arrived for the Scotts, in the form of an accident. In February 1916 on the Dubin Docks, a hawser broke, and my great-grandfather William Scott was thrown into the River Liffey between a dredger and the dock. He died some days later in hospital from pneumonia. Two months later, during the Rising, Annie Scott, who was now a single parent to six children, took her second youngest child, Walter Scott, out to look for food. They were both caught in gun fire which, according to family lore, came from the gunship *Helga* which was shelling City Hall. Annie was shot in the leg and Walter, who was eight years old, in the head. He died two months later in hospital. Annie Scott would get a small grant as a victim of the Rebellion, a grant that was cut from £25 to £10 by a mean-spirited civil servant. To support herself she became an agent for the Royal Liver Assurance Company.

## Signing up

Granddad enlisted in 1918, just weeks after his 19th birthday. Perhaps the reason for signing up at 19 was because he was more likely to be sent straight overseas. It may seem unusual for a young man who was familiar with streets where workers had been baton-charged by British soldiers in 1913 and who lost a brother to a rebellion that was quashed by British soldiers in those same streets, to sign up with the British Army. However at least 200,000 Irishmen signed up to the British Army between August of 1914 and November 1918 over 28,000 of those recruited in Dublin. 8000 of their number would not come home. Many of those young men could not afford the luxury of principles. Later, ex-British soldiers like my granddad would be accepted into both the Free State Army and the IRA. And ex-British soldiers would fight on both sides of the Irish Civil War. (East Wall for All, 2017) (McGreevy, 2014).

His personal reasons we can only guess at. Before joining the army, he was serving an apprenticeship at a jeweller's shop in Dublin and perhaps the intricate, indoor work seemed stultifying to a young man whose life had already been darkened by tragedy. Certainly, from his subsequent career it's hard to imagine this profession would have suited him. He was more of a man of action, interested in being out and about 'doing' rather than sitting in a workshop or office. My father contrasts his thoughts during his own training in the British Army in the 1950's with the attitude of his father…

*'We were bayonet training, fixing bayonets at the correct angle and running at straw men, stabbing them, withdrawing to run to the next one, again to stab when it hit me properly that I was being trained to kill and it shook me. He [Gerald] would not have had those thoughts.*

His eldest son, my late uncle Billy, would similarly sign up for the Palestine Police Force in 1947 at the age of 18 on seeing an ad in the papers promising adventure (and money). Billy too was a 'man of action', naturally skilled with the fishing rod, rifle and catapult, in fact any physical activity he put his hand to. Granddad was a just young man without political ideals and with very simple and common motivators: economics, youth and a desire for action.

## Churchill & the Bolsheviks

Meanwhile, there had been a Bolshevik Revolution in Russia in 1917. Or strictly two: the February Revolution, when the Tsar Nicholas abdicated, and the October one after which Lenin's Bolsheviks were in charge. A civil war ensued among the various factions, some of whom received outside help. Bolshevism was seen in the west as barbaric and a threat to the foundations of

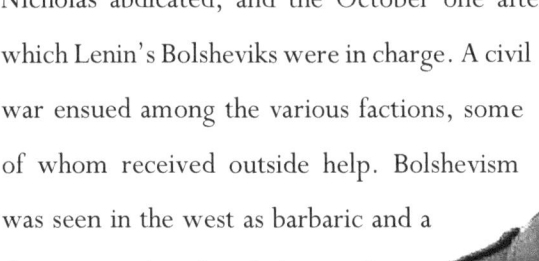

FIG. 2. WINSTON CHURCHILL OCTOBER 1918. SOURCE: IMPERIAL WAR MUSEUM.

civilisation but despite the unpopularity of communism, Winston Churchill, British Secretary of State for Air and later also the Secretary of State for War, faced strong opposition from a war-weary government - particularly Prime Minister Lloyd George – when he began to push for aid for the White Army fighting the Bolsheviks. Churchill's obsession with beating the 'Bolshies' was, and still is, incomprehensible to many and would impact his career already damaged by his involvement in the disastrous Dardanelles campaign. Churchill was not to be discouraged and began organising the expeditionary force in 1918 though he would only receive cabinet go-ahead in spring 1919 and with sparse support. A British expeditionary force would be attached in a loose alliance to the Tsarists, represented by the White Army, and war materiel left over from The Great War would be made available. It was then that there was a call put out for volunteers and an increased rate of pay was offered. Granddad, probably training in the UK at this point, volunteered for the Mission in April 1919. There were British soldiers in a number of areas in Russia but South Russia was the base for the Volunteer Army and later The White Army and from where they struck out for Moscow. It was through South Russia the Whites – and millions of civilians - were routed. It was to South Russia that granddad was headed.

route for Fran
arrived at Bou
-pm on the so
e. We stopped t
Column Camp (St.
rtin's) and entr
9-30 pm. on Sa
Nov. 1919. en-r
Marseilles. We
pped at the foll
the journey, Am
is, Di-jon, Avi
rles and after
s train journ

*"We left Wendover at 1:30pm on Thursday 30th Oct. 1919 and arrived at Dover at 8:30pm on the same date."*

This is the first line of my grandfather's account. In my naivety I had thought we would just embark and head off over the ocean waves, the cliffs of Dover fading into the distance, Russia a paragraph away, but immediately I had questions. Why Wendover? How did he get there?

It was likely he joined the army in Dublin and was then sent to the UK for training. His departure point of Wendover in Buckinghamshire is the nearest depot to the Royal Air Force (RAF) training centre of Halton which began operations in 1913. Halton was also a technical training school for mechanics and by 1917 there were 10,000 trainees there (and I assume support staff) including 2000 women and 2000 boys. Granddad was not a pilot, or a mechanic and I don't know if the RAF was his choice. Of his time there, there is no mention.

Wendover - meaning white waters which owes something to the chalk in the surrounding hills - is apparently very picturesque. It was once home to William the Conqueror and the Boleyns but I imagine a nineteen-year-old man on the brink of his first big adventure, didn't care much about that. Through France

*"We spent that night at N0.2 Rest Camp and embarked at 12 noon on Friday 31st Oct.1919 on "The Maid of Orleans" en-route for France. We arrived at Boulogne at 2pm on the same date. We stopped that night at Column Camp (St. Martin's) and entrained at 9:30pm on Sat. 1st Nov. 1919 en-route for Marseilles."*

## The Maid of Orleans

The Maid of Orleans, which brought granddad from Dover to Boulogne, was ordered by Southeast and Chatham Railways and the keel was laid in 1914 in Dumbarton, coincidentally my granddad's birthplace. Converted to a troopship with capacity for 1,000 soldiers in 1917 and launched in 1918, the Maid carried Mahatma Gandhi to Britain for government talks in 1919 - he refused a cabin and squatted in third class - the same year my grandfather and his unit were ferried across the channel. Winston Churchill was also, briefly, a passenger in 1943. Most of her life was spent carrying civilian passengers across the channel, however she was converted once more for use as a troopship at the onset of the Second World War and was sunk northeast of Barfleur as she returned from her sixth voyage to Dunkirk with the loss of five crew. 92 survivors were picked up. Nowadays when we sail to France it is Cherbourg, near Barfleur, where ships dock.

FIG. 3. THE MAID OF ORLEANS, 1920, FROM THE ROY THORNTON COLLECTION. THORNTON, GOODFELLOW, 1913.

FIG. 4.   REST CAMP NO.3 ON THE LEAS IN FOLKESTONE. SOURCE: DOVER AND FOLKESTONE DURING THE GREAT WAR, BARNSLEY: PEN & SWORD MILITARY, GEORGE, 2008.

## Rest Camps

The network of rest camps in the U.K. and beyond was very familiar to the troops as way stations on much travelled routes. To young men on their first trip abroad they served as stepping-stones through foreign lands which also shielded the men from the temptations of different cultures. A Rest Camp was simply a camp where soldiers could be housed together while waiting to depart for war, or a place of 'rest' from battle. They were often situated in large houses or hotels. There were three in the environs of Dover, called, in prosaic army fashion, 1, 2, and 3. The camps had beds, canteens and shops where everything from sweetheart brooches to powder to combat trench foot could be bought. At the

Great War's peak, 10,000 men a day passed through the camps. Most soldiers were given a Bible or a Book of Psalms on departing. The rest camp which granddad refers to as Column Camp, or St. Martin's, is near Boulogne in an area known as Osterhove, once a village now an area to the west of Boulogne's centre. Incidentally at Osterhove there is a well that used to serve an ancient leper colony in nearby La Madeline so the site of the camps there - there were at least five, St. Martins' being No.2 - overlaid the ghostly foundations of successive institutions stretching back centuries.

*"We stopped at the following stations on the journey, Amiens, Paris, Di-jon, Avignon & Arles and after 48 hours train journey we finished up at L'Staque and marched from there to N0.10 Rest Camp, Marseilles. We arrived at the Rest Camp at 8:30pm on Monday 3rd Nov. 1919. We spent two days in Marseilles and had a real good time."*

I travelled in France when I was younger, taking the high-speed TGV from Paris to Toulouse. While my route was were parallel to granddad's 70 years earlier, I did not pass through the same stations he did. I found a lot to wonder at as I stared out at the towns, villages, and countryside; strange beer signs, cobblestone streets, fields of rapeseed, avenues of trees, houses with old beams inset into warm, coloured plaster, villages perched on the hills of the Central Massif. By contrast, granddad, forty-eight hours on a train through a foreign country for the first time in his life, makes no mention of the landscape, towns or villages or people. They cannot have gone unnoticed but was perhaps seemed of little importance later when he came to write about the journey. Perhaps, travelling in a group, stopping off at well-established camps with familiar names, the soldiers existed in a bubble that protected them from anything strange or different and focussed them on the task at hand. But, as my father mentioned, granddad was not given much to pondering, which will become apparent as we progress. While writing this, I realised that my rucksack at the time was an army issue duffel bag. It has little meaning but it's a symmetry I appreciate. Unlike granddad, I ponder quite a bit.

L'Estaque - L'Staque as my grandfather wrote it - was where the train journey ended. It is a place familiar to many because it was painted many times by the artist Paul Cezanne whose work sprang to mind when I saw L'Staque written in faded ink in grandad's little notebook. Cezanne died in 1906. Granddad was a lot closer in time to Cezanne than we are, shared the same world even. It is with Cezanne's eyes that I look through on rich warm days by the shore when the sea is a solid block of the most startling ultramarine. It is quite a visual jump from speckled brown pages to the shores of a foreign sea, but it is this sort of contrast that first snagged my imagination and made me attempt this colouring in my grandad's account of his long-ago journey.

Rest Camp No.10 near Marseille was about a mile and a half from the port according to the diary of one William James Cording who passed through there in July of 1919. Cording's diary is a bit chattier than my granddad's account and his emphasis is slightly different. Cording's unit caught a tram into Marseille town one day. He described it merely as 'very nice' though, 'everything was dear'.

*"Everything was green and beautiful about and plenty of fruit about which we 'ad a good feed oft, we 'ad plenty of pears which we picked from the trees".*

He likes his food does Cording. He writes that the rations were far better than they had at Port Said (where granddad would also travel through) and later, on leaving Marseille, he again writes about how green and beautiful everything was with, again, *'plenty of fruit about'*.

The difference between granddads and Cording's accounts is perhaps not only indicative of two different personalities but of the difference between a diary written day-to-day and an account written after the fact. Details like pear trees and green countryside might slip the mind a year and an expedition later. Still, Cording's Marseille sounds like an English country village, a place of bounty (and expensive goods) unlike the Marseille of lore, a port town, geographically and politically a place on the edge, a Wild West on a sea that for much of history was a highway for armies, pirates, slavers and every sort of human flotsam and jetsam. My granddad's brief *'We had a real good time'* while low on detail, seems more in keeping with what a unit of soldiers might get up to in a port town than Cording's ode to orchards.

...ere to No. 10 Rest
...mp, Marseilles. We
...rived at the Rest
...mp at 8-30 pm on
...nday 3rd Nov. 1919.
...ent two days in
...arseilles & had a ...
...od time. We saile...
...om Marseilles on ...
...M. T. Porto en-rou...
... for Constantinop...
...a Malta & Moudro...
...eece.) at 2 pm on
...hursday 6th Nov. 1...
... passed the coa...
...Corsica & Sardin...

# Chapter Two: Here be Monsters

## Into the Mediterranean

*"We sailed from Marseilles on the "H.M.S Porto" en-route for Constantinople via Malta & Moudros (Greece) at 2pm on Thursday 6th Nov. 1919. We passed the coast of Corsica & Sardinia at 10pm on Friday 7th Nov. 1919. Corsica is an island near Italy where Napoleon was born."*

The mention of Napoleon is a reminder of the different cultural and historical landscape my granddad occupied. He did not know of Hitler, Mussolini, Stalin, Mao Tse Tung, or Pol Pot. The scale of the atrocity of the Great War may not have had time to sink into the collective consciousness and Napoleon Bonaparte, who had dominated global affairs for the first decade of the 1800's, still loomed large in my granddad's cultural vocabulary. As it happens some of Bonaparte's relatives are buried in Waterford city in the southeast of Ireland. Granddad would settle in the county next door, by the sea, while my father, born in Waterford's Comeragh Mountains, would settle in Waterford.

*"We saw a whale spouting at 12-noon on Sat. 8th Nov. 1919. At 9:30pm on the same date we passed the coast of Sicily on which is the volcano "Etna" which destroyed Messina by its tremendous flow of lava in the year 1908."*

Granddad more than likely will have heard tales about whales and other sea creatures on the Dublin docks where his father, my great-grandfather, worked. From the banks of the Clyde to the port of Dublin to the deck of a ship in the Mediterranean and down through the years, to his lengthiest posting as Garda in Baldwinstown in South Wexford and his last home near the Quay in Wexford town, the sea was always familiar.

It is a great thing to see a whale. The force of blow explodes into the air followed by the rolling black back wreathed in rainbows. There are smiles all around and camaraderie blossoms. For the men on the *Porto,* it must have been a welcome break in an anxious journey. It is likely he saw a Sperm Whale or a Fin Whale, the second biggest mammal in the world and the ones I see most often from my house near the sea. Between 1921 and 1954 many fin whales were captured in a vigorous period of whaling in that area so the animal he saw probably met with a sticky end.

# H.M.S Porto

The *Porto* was once a German ship called the *Prinz Heinrich* after the crown prince. There are lots of *Prinz Heinrich*s, including an armoured cruiser of roughly the same vintage, but the one granddad travelled on is a steam ship built for cargo and/or passengers. Built in Danzig in 1894, rebuilt in 1909 to 6636 tons the *Prinz Heinrich* was interned at Lisbon at the outbreak of the Great War and seized and renamed *Porto* by the Portuguese. She was ceded to the British at the end of the war and then sublet to the Hudson Bay Company and employed on the Hamburg to Buenos Aires service. Withdrawn as too old fashioned in 1924 the *Porto* was broken up in Italy in 1925. The Mediterranean was not the normal stomping ground (if ships stomp) during this period. For instance, the *Porto* had brought the No.1 Middlesex Special Company, for the North Russia Expeditionary Force, to Murmansk from Tilbury in April 1919.

FIG.5 PORTO AS THE PRINZ HEINRICH FROM EDWIN DRECHSEL IN NORDDEUTSCHER LLOYD, BREMEN: 1857-1970 VOL. I (CORDILLERA PUBLISHING CO., VANCOUVER 1994).

## Etna & the Messina Disaster

Etna is one of the most active volcanoes in Europe, a designation which has as much to do with lava emissions as explosive eruptions. I stood on the slopes of Mount Etna seven decades after granddad had passed by it, watching the lava smoke, in no danger except perhaps of getting sunburned. Though Etna had erupted in April 1908, a worse disaster that year was the earthquake of December 28th, the biggest disaster in European history. Measuring 7.1 on

**FIG.6 STREET IN MESSINA, SICILY, SHOWING DAMAGE CAUSED BY THE EARTHQUAKE, JANUARY 1909. COLLECTION OF LIEUTENANT COMMANDER RICHARD WAINWRIGHT, 1928.**

the Richter scale it created a 40-foot-high tsunami. In a city whose hotels were packed for a performance of Aida between 70,000 and 100,000 people died while others were buried alive up to a week or more. 90% of buildings in Messina were destroyed. Fifty years on there were still people living in make-shift housing. All the municipal records were destroyed. There was a massive increase in emigration after the quake and the departure of much of the male population contributed to the death of many villages on the island and consequently the rise of the Mafia in North America.

Granddad was only nine years old in 1908 and the news from Messina, which must have been discussed among adults, may have become entwined with the imagery of other disasters, and perhaps compared with the eruption of Krakatoa, far away in the Pacific, in 1883, in the time of my great-grandparents. That eruption was felt around the globe. There was a world-wide wave of atmospheric pressure creating spectacular sunsets over the following eighteen months which influenced paintings such as Munch's *The Scream*. There was also a longer lasting wave, one of information. Krakatoa was the first disaster of its kind to be telegraphed around the world. The suffering of people far away could be empathized with, something new for those who were not yet overwhelmed by super-charged media. For the first time events were instantly reported before mythologized versions provided coping mechanisms for the psyche. The wonder of the whale, Etna, the terrible disaster at Messina hint at depths beneath the surface of the faded pages. Though he was a markedly unemotional and pragmatic man, it is hard not to see the spouting leviathan and the exploding volcano forming a gateway into the unknown, a passage from the fantasy of adventure to real life war.

### Malta

*"We arrived at Malta at 2pm on Sunday 9th Nov. 1919. We went ashore & had a jolly time. When our ship entered the harbour of Malta a large number of small boats came all round our ship, the boatmen of which were trying to sell us different things such as fags, fruit, chocolate & silks. There were other small boats around us in which there were boys & also young men absolutely naked who were diving for pieces of silver which were being thrown to them from our ship. It was very amusing to watch them. These lads are born swimmers. These boats which come round a ship on her entrance to the harbour are commonly known as bum-boats. The language spoken is mostly English as Malta is a British possession and there are a great number of English people living there. A Maltese woman wears a big black hood on her head. Malta itself is a beautiful place."*

Some of the more detailed observations granddad makes throughout the diary are from the times he was on board a ship. This entry is the first one of real colour. Perhaps life might have seemed richer with the campaign in Russia looming. *The Porto* was moored no doubt in one of Valletta's lovely harbours that lie beneath the high, ochre yellow walls that rise from the intense ultramarine and turquoise of the Mediterranean.

Malta was a British satellite and way station during the World Wars. It has always been hugely strategically important though during the Great War Malta merely served as a replenishing and refuelling depot and a hospital for troops. It is also a very beautiful place. Walking the streets of Valletta, the sea is visible from every point on the narrow streets that drop down to the massive walls. Many soldiers would have passed through here on their way to and from theatres of war. The aforementioned W.J. Cording passed through in 1916 and also experienced the boats of the Maltese...

*'In Malta, April 7th. We are making for the dock and it is much calmer. As we go inland...there is a big hospital boat there. Everything is very interesting. Any amount of small boats is around us..*

He writes of the beauty of the island and the frustration of not being allowed onshore.

*'We are still at Malta. It is a lovely day and there is lovely to see all around. We are close to French War ships. It seems jolly hard to have to stay on the boat as we should like to land and have a look around. The natives are all around us.'*

Cording was there for four or five days, all spent on board. My granddad, who was only there one day, was lucky to get onshore but the natural topography of the harbour meant even from the water there would have been plenty to see. The massive walls pocked and yellow in the sun, the buildings, domes, low towers, spires and arches, houses in crumbling sandstone, boxy bay windows and signs with peeling paint leaning over steep cobbled streets, people walking to and fro in the city and under the walls where the fishermen have their shacks the cats prowl for titbits.

Despite the 'jolly time' my grandad had onshore, it is the boats and the brown, lithe swimmers cleaving the turquoise waters of the harbour that leave the greatest splash of colour on the minds' eye. The blue, yellow and white painted traditional boats that surrounded my granddad's ship take their colours from the surrounding sea and sky and the rocky sandstone of this tiny island nation.

The scattering of money to watch boys diving recalls to mind a Scottish boy I saw once outside a shop in a tiny, impoverished village in Namibia. He was amusing himself by flinging coins on the ground so he could watch local children scrabble in the dust for them. The colonialist attitudes the Empire bred were deeply embedded, even in those under its yoke, especially in the army, and continue to this day.

*The Ghonella* or the 'big hood' that the Maltese women wore was also called a *Faldetta*. It was traditional Maltese dress dating back to the time of the Knights of Malta. It was worn by noble women to denote modesty. A bit roomier than the bourka, it looks like an umbrella or a small porch. Meghan Markle, who has Maltese ancestry, wore one during a visit to Malta in 2015.

## Lemnos & Moudros

*"We left Malta at 8am on Monday 10th Nov. 1919. We had a concert on the ship on the 11th Nov. 1919 in commemoration of the signing of the Armistice. We entered the Aegean Sea at 9am on Wednesday the 12th Nov. 1919 & we also arrived among the many islands of the Grecian Archipelago at the same time on the same date. We arrived at Moudross which is a town on an island called Lemnos Island and which is one of the many islands which comprise the Grecian Archipelago, at 9am on Thursday 13th Nov. 1919 & left at 2pm on the same date."*

During the concert, it was likely there was the obligatory two-minute silence, but he does not mention it, leaving the only the imagined cacophonous clash of drums and cymbals echoing in opposition to the near global respectful silence that was offered on that day. Back then, an individual's thoughts on the first anniversary of that unprecedented and vast slaughter would probably have been considered somewhat irrelevant. It is probable too that most people would not have had the language to describe it and perhaps there was an eagerness to leave it behind.

Lemnos, also known as Limnos, is in the armpit of Greece, and its history reflects its position on the border between east and west. It was a province of the Byzantine Empire, apportioned to the Latin

Empire for much of the 13th century, ceded back to Byzantium in 1277 and became a part of the Ottoman Empire. In 1912 it became part of Greece and remains so today. It is small with a current population of just under 17,000. In 1915 Lemnos had served as a base for the Gallipoli campaign and as such has significance for Australia who lost so many men there. The town of Lemnos in Victoria, Australia (current pop. 369), established in 1927 as a soldier settlement zone for those returning from the Great War, was named after the island and still maintains connections with it. Paintings of Lemnos from this time convey little of the colour of the Greek islands. Though Cezanne and Van Gogh were already dead and Picasso well into his career, the vibrant colours and energy of those artists would not yet have been common visual currency. It is interesting to think then that it is not only the old photographs that make the past seem black and white but that all forms of visual media back then tended towards the dull, the staid, the conservative. For my granddad, getting closer to his destination, the one thing that caught his eye in Lemnos was a Bolshevik ship run aground. It would have brought home the reality of the conflict that he was heading into.

*"On entering Moudross harbour we saw a Bolshevik ship, which was used as a gunrunner, lying on the rocks with her back broken. She was being chased by one of our destroyers*

*and she tried to cross some submerged rocks but she struck them and was wrecked."*

It is impossible to find out which ship this was. With the Russian Civil War, the Russian Navy had disintegrated. A 'Bolshevik ship' might not necessarily have previously sailed under the flag of the Russian Imperial Navy and even if it had its name might have changed. Likewise, a 'gunrunner' can mean any sort of boat that was used to smuggle guns. If the sight of her broken on the rocks was taken as a good omen by those going to fight the Bolsheviks, that omen carried false promise.

...d Dervishes for...
...n of forty piast[res]
...se Dervishes danc[e]
...mselves into a fren[zy]
...madness & then t[he]
...ead priest start[s]
...ving nails throug[h]
...is cheeks & stiche[s]
...is lips together &
...es other terrible t[hings]
...them. It is a kin[d of]
...religious ceremony &
...ay tell you it is [a]
...ight you dont wa[nt to]
...see a second ti[me]

# Chapter Three: Constantinople

## At the Gates of War

*"We entered the Dardanelles at 7pm on the same date (Thursday 13th November 1919). We dropped anchor for the night outside Chanak as it was too dangerous to proceed any further in the dark. At 9am on Friday 14th Nov. 1919 we passed three ships which had been sunk by shell fire, lying close to the shore. These ships I believe were sunk within a period of five minutes. At 5am we passed Gallipoli and entered the Sea of Marmara at 6pm on the same date."*

The Dardanelles Strait with the Gallipoli peninsula to the west and mainland Turkey to the east, at nearly 70km long, connects the Aegean with The Sea of Marmara. The Ottomans had begun mining the straits on their entrance into the Great War at the end of 1914 and there were reports of Turkish artillery on land. The ships my granddad mentions in his diary entry would have probably been the French battleship *Bouvet* which supposedly struck a mine in 1915, causing her to capsize in two minutes, with just 75 survivors out of a total crew of 718, and the *HMS Irresistible* from which most of the surviving crew were rescued; *HMS Ocean* sent to rescue *Irresistible*, struck a mine, and was abandoned, eventually to sink. Some of these mines would no doubt have still been about. At Chanak the strait narrows to only 1.6km. It was a key point which the Allied powers tried to control to establish a route to Constantinople, and so to Russia, during the Great War, in order to divert the Ottoman's campaign in The Caucasus. They launched a naval attack on the Gallipoli Peninsula - for which Winston Churchill bore partial responsibility - but after eight months of fighting were defeated by the Ottomans in 1915 with disastrous losses on both sides. Given the limited geography there would have been much evidence of this great battle still about and no doubt if would have resonance for the soldiers on the *Porto* only four years on.

## Constantinople

*"We arrived at Constantinople at 11pm on the same date & dropped anchor in the harbour for the night. We landed in Constantinople at 12 noon on Sat. 15th Nov. after 9 days at sea. We arrived at Maslak Rest Camp at 4pm on the same date. We spent close on a month in Constantinople & and on the day before we embarked for Russia we visited Mosque St. Sophie which is the oldest mosque in the world & and we also visited the world famous bazaar in Stamboul."*

The Constantinople that the *Porto* stopped off at, for eons a crucial point between east and west, was the spinning centre of one of the deeper eddies of its history, one of many swirling around the ravenous whirlpool that was Great War. For the first time since the city had fallen to the Turk in 1453, it was occupied by foreign powers: the British primarily but also the French and Italians. Turkey had entered World War I on the side of the Germans having previously been involved in the First and Second Balkan Wars (1912 and 1913 respectively). In the first, Turkey lost badly against an Alliance including Greece, Austria, and Bulgaria, ceding the last of their European territory. The Second Balkan War was over the division of the spoils of the previous one. It was in large part the tensions of these conflicts which led to the Great War. The Armistice of Moudros, which ended the Ottoman involvement in the war on October 30th 1918, came with the condition that the Allies could occupy the city for security reasons. The British would eventually dismantle the apparatus of the Ottoman Empire, disempowering the Sultan by separating him from his parliament and inadvertently galvanizing the Turkish National Movement, catapulting the country into the Turkish War of Independence. Mustapha Kemal or Ataturk, who emerged as a brilliant leader during Turkey's victory at Gallipoli, led the Nationalists or The Young Turks, a political reform movement that consisted of Ottoman exiles, students, civil servants, and army officers. The British backed the Ottoman Empire by supporting guerrilla groups - which included refugees from the Russian Civil War - as well as the Ottoman security army, Kuva-i-inzibatiye, which come into being months later on April 18th 1920. But the British quickly realised they were not prepared to launch the type of offensive which would bring down the revolution and by the end of June 1920 the Kuva-i-inzibatiye would be dismantled with many of those men joining the Nationalists. The last Ottoman Sultan, Mehmed VI, would leave the city in a British ship in 1922. Granddad would leave Constantinople in the first week of December 1919 when the last elections of the Ottoman Empire were held. These elections saw the ascent of many Nationalists including Ataturk, to the last parliament, convened in January 1920 before Ataturk rebooted it in Ankara in 1923. Granddad would be once again in the city during April 1920 when the security forces were being mustered for that Civil War. Both times he was in Constantinople it was at vital points in the city's history and though these events are not mentioned what we do get in my granddad's account is a flash of colour a thumbnail sketch of a world on the brink.

## St. Sophie

*"On entering Mosque St. Sophie an attendant at the door gives you a pair of slippers to put over your boots so as you won't break some act of their religion by walking in the mosque with dirty boots on. A Turk before he enters takes off his boots and washes his feet & then goes in barefooted. On coming out the door keeper charges you five piastres for the use of the slippers."*

St. Sophia was founded by the Roman Emperor Justinian in 537 A.D. as a church for the Byzantine Court. When the Turk conquered Constantinople in 1453, St. Sophia became the Hagia Sophia, a mosque and so it remained until it was converted into a museum by Ataturk in 1934. Muslims have long been agitating to have it reinstated as a mosque and though the Turkish leader Recep Tayyip Erdogan, suggested that other mosques in the city should be filled first, in 2020, in a move that pleased his conservative supporters but dismayed the rest of the world, Erdogan declared St. Sophie a mosque once more.

**"*An Armenian will not be allowed to enter Mosque St. Sophie by the Turkish soldiers at entrance to the mosque.*"**

Armenia, a country to the east of Turkey between the Black and Caspian Seas and the Ottoman Empire had been, during most of its history, a part of either the Ottoman Empire or that of Iran. It had also been the first nation to declare itself as Christian in the early 4th century. When it eventually began to fight for more freedom from the strict Muslim rule of the Turk in the late 19th century, being stuck between the crumbling Ottoman Empire and

the crumbling Russian Empire was a bad place to be. The Ottoman Sultan Hamid II initiated what would become known as the Hamidian Massacres which killed between 80,000 and 300,000 Armenians in the 1890s. But that was small potatoes. The

Ottomans became suspicious (or perhaps we should say, increasingly suspicious) of the Armenians at the outbreak of the Great War because some had volunteered for the Imperial Russian Army which was in alliance with Britain and France against Germany who Turkey had allied with.

The Armenians became victim to what is considered to be the first modern genocide which kicked off in May of 1915 when Armenian intellectuals were arrested. Massacres of able-bodied men, forced death marches into the desert for the elderly and infirm and labour camps followed. The death toll is said to have been between 1 and 1.5 million.

FIG.7 AN ARMENIAN, SCRIBNER'S 1893, COLLECTION OF MAGGIE LAND BLANCK. SOURCE: WWW.MAGGIEBLANCK.COM, 2012.

It is surprising there were any Armenians left in Constantinople and even more surprising that any might try to get into The Hagia Sophia. This genocide has had far reaching effects, but it was only in April of 2021 that President Biden finally acknowledged it under long pressure from Armenians in the U.S. and elsewhere.

*"The city of Constantinople is very picturesque, but the side lanes are very dirty and the streets are badly paved. While we were there, there were certain parts of the city which were out of bounds to British troops owing to an outbreak of bubonic plague."*

Though the Bubonic Plague or Black Death is commonly said to have originated in the 14th century - possibly in China like our current pandemic - a much earlier pandemic, originating in Constantinople in 542AD, which killed between 30 and 50 million across the known world, was said to be related to it. 'Justinian's plague' was due to Justinian's expansion into Africa to bring orthodox Christians back under the protection of the empire. The outbreak of plague in 1919 occurred soon after the British Occupation, between September 1919 and January 1920. It originated near the city granary. It only infected 54 and killed 19, due to better knowledge of the disease, advances in medicine and, improved infrastructure. Plague would break out again in April 1920 when granddad was once again in the city when further 56 were infected. My granddad and his unit would be quarantined for most of his month-long stay in April 2020 because of a typhus outbreak.

FIG.8. (OVERLEAF) GALATA BRIDGE, CONSTANTINOPLE, DECEMBER 5TH, 1919. PHOTO GEORGE SWAIN. SOURCE: THE DOCUMENTARY IMAGINATION (PART TWO), A DAY'S JOURNEY: CONSTANTINOPLE DECEMBER 9TH 1919, IN THE MICHIGAN QUARTERLY REVIEW, VOL. XLV, ISSUE 1, WINTER 2006.

## A Day Out

In 1919 there also arrived in Constantinople an historian and his photographer looking for manuscripts which often come on the market in times of war. Francis W. Kelsey was a professor of languages at Michigan University, and he had hired George Swain as driver and photographer (a necessity for manuscript hunters to record manuscripts). Their attention became diverted from the ancient manuscripts to the 'explosive present' of the city.

The result is a series of candid photographs of early 20th century Constantinople. The photographs are from between the 4th to the 18th of December 1919. This image is of the Galata Bridge which leads directly to the Grand Bazaar on December 5th, the day my grandad also visited the Bazaar as well as Saint Sophia. It is curious to think they might have passed each other on the street, that granddad could have been snapped as he went about the city.

## The Mad Dervishes

*"You can also see on Fridays only the Mad Dervishes for the sum of forty piastres. These Dervishes dance themselves into a frenzy of madness & the head priest starts driving nails through their cheeks & sticks their lips together & also does other terrible things to them. It is a kind of religious ceremony & I may tell you it is a sight you don't want to see a second time."*

Friday is an important day in Islam. The prophet Muhammed said there is no day more important than Friday and one of the greatest verses of the Koran were revealed on a Friday.

*"This day, I have perfected your religion for you, completed My Favor upon you, and have chosen Islam as your religion." (Quran 5:3).*

Dervishes, of whom there are hundreds of orders throughout Islam's history, come under the umbrella of Sufism, the mystical end of that religion. Sufism was often frowned upon by ordinary Muslims. The Sufi saint and poet Rumi did much to bring knowledge of Sufism and thus the dervishes to the world. The word *dervish* comes from the Persian word for 'sill of the door' *darvish*, and their practices are described as being the door to enlightenment. I had assumed granddad's dervishes were Whirling Dervishes whose spinning hypnotic dance is said to bring them closer to God. However, images and videos of elegantly spinning practitioners, heads tilted, eyes closed, twirling in their halo-like white skirts, did not seem that 'mad'. Further research revealed that dervishes are divided into lodges or tekkes - which also describes the buildings that house the dervishes. One lodge, the Qalandar, or Kalandar, a sect of wandering dervishes, was welcomed by Turkish nomads around the 12th century. The

Qalandar were anarchists who believed music, wine, buggery and opium smoking would bring them closer to God. They rejected and criticised material wealth. This made them unpopular, but they would have a great influence on Turkish Islam and eventually be absorbed into other tekkes. The Qalandar influence could still be seen in the wilder practices of the Howling Dervishes, or the Bektashi Rifa'i or Rufa'i sect. Physical trials were said to be the triumph of the spirit over the flesh and various exercises included putting iron rings in hands, necks, ears and even their 'male members' to prevent them having intercourse. This last example was probably one of the *'other terrible things'* that my granddad mentioned beyond the piercing of cheeks and lips. Other descriptions of ceremonies describe juggling and swallowing swords and fire, dancing in grotesque positions as well as instruments like spikes, chains, and pincers.

Samuel Anderson, in his 1923 book *The Whirling and Howling Dervishes*, wrote an account of a visit to see the Howling Dervishes in Constantinople in 1921. He paid a mere 20 piastres to granddads' 40 piastres two years previously but then he wasn't at St. Sophia, and he wasn't a soldier of an occupying force. The Whirling Dervishes and the Howling Dervishes were, and are, the two tekkes that stage *zikr* for outsiders though they were often shorter ceremonies than the private ones. All Dervish lodges would be banned in Atatürk's' new secular republic in 1925 but the dervishes survived. Today the Bektashi still exist in the Balkans as well as in the U.S. Sufism has enjoyed something of a revival. The day after granddad saw the dervish ritual, traditionally a means to ramp up aggression as a prelude to war, he embarked for South Russia and what was already the rout of The White Army.

am on Sat. 6th D
and sailed for
Russia at 4 pm o
same date. We
ropped anchor in
sphorous for that
ght & sailed a
7 am next morn
w. 7th Dec 1919. W
tered the Black
9 am on the s
te. The following
otice appeared
ships orders
same date, —

# Chapter Four: Into the Black Sea

*Into a minefield & Wexford*

*"We embarked on the "H.M.S. Huntscastle" at 11am on Sat. 6th Dec. 1919 and sailed for Russia at 4 pm on the same date. We dropped anchor in the Bosphorus for that night and sailed again at 7am next morning Sun. 7th Dec. 1919. We entered the Black Sea at 9am on the same date. The following notice appeared in the ships orders on the same date - all men must be ready to turn out fully armed at a moments notice to fire on floating mines."*

The Dardanelles had recently been mined by the Ottoman Army, but granddad had not mentioned them when he passed through. In the Black Sea they were obviously more of a threat. The floating mines were most likely the M-08 which was developed in 1908 in the Russia of Tsar Nicholas II. The M-08 is the classic spiky black ball, a design which is still the most widespread worldwide. They had to be chained to the sea floor, so they were usually found in shallow water. As they were crude, their effectiveness depended on quantity not quality. They were more than likely laid by the Russian army prior to the 1917 revolution when they blockaded the Turkish Coast near the Bosphorus and Varna (Bulgaria) in 1915 and 1916.

# The Huntscastle

The *Huntscastle* started life in 1902 as a cargo ship named *Louisiana*. 127.1 m long, with a capability of 12 knots, she could carry 100 passengers in three classes. In 1905 she was purchased from Argo Shipping of Bremen by the Woermann Line of Hamburg and renamed *Erna Woermann*, the second of that name. The *Erna Woermann* was used as a transport for troops dealing with the Herero uprising of 1904 through 1907 and would have moored often in Swakopmund where the Woerman Line had facilities. Having spent time once in Swakopmund and around Okahandja, home to the Herero, it is mind boggling that armed troops were shipped out there 100 years ago to deal with what seemed even in the 21st century to be a simple rural tribe. In 1914 the *Erma Woermann* was captured by the British in Douala, Cameroon. Renamed *Huntscastle*, she was used as a troop transport and cargo ship, carrying my granddad to South Russia in 1919. In 1921 she was sold to German East Africa Line renamed *Sultan* and operated on a round Africa route. She was scrapped in 1933.

It would be another two decades before granddad's closest and most dangerous encounter with a mine which occurred when he was a member of the Irish Police, the Garda Siochana. He was stationed in Baldwinstown, a small village in Wexford, from June 1940 until his retirement in 1962. Near Baldwinstown at Cullenstown Strand, there is a small estuary that runs parallel to the sea but divided from it by a spit of land forming a long bay locally called The Cull. In January 1941 a floating mine washed up on the shore at The Cull. Thirty mines, most likely British, had already come ashore during the last days of that January, probably the result of winter storms. These mines were very volatile but not easily disarmed so the Gardaí would call in the Local Defence Force (LDF). When they arrived, they made attempts to detonate the mine by shooting at it - the same method ordered on the H.M.S. *Huntscastle* in 1919 - with .303 rifles but failed. They concluded that they needed to secure it as the tide came up and someone was dispatched to find some more rope. In the meantime, the remaining LDF men had another go at disarming the mine. Granddad was sheltering behind a hedge with the local schoolmaster from Duncormick when the mine exploded, killing three men instantly. The fourth died some days later. There was a commemoration for the soldiers in 2010.

## Trebizon and Batoum

*"We arrived at Trebizon which is in Armenia in the continent of Asia at 10am on Tuesday 9th Dec. 1919 & sailed again at 4pm on the same date. We at arrived Batoum (Russia) at 11am Wed. 10th Dec. 1919. We stayed at Batoum for two days & had a good look round the town. It is a very small place. You can see the whole town in three or four hours."*

In the 1400s Trebizond was the last great trading outpost of the west but had since declined. Batoum had more recently flourished after the oil boom of the 1890s. On the sea and surrounded by the Caucasus Mountains, it was frequented by many wealthy people including the Rothschilds and the Swedish brothers Nobel. By the time my granddad got there though, Batoum had already begun to turn into an isolated backwater. Flash forward a century and Batumi (Bat'umi), pop, 150,000, with its deep-sea port is now one of the principal cities in Georgia. The Rose Revolution in 2003 - named for the roses brandished by the peaceful revolutionaries -

ousted the communist party leader along with the climate of corruption, introducing a progressive leadership which has transformed the region. Due to the ban on gambling in surrounding nations the wealthy go to Bat'umi to gamble, and it is once again an internationally popular resort. The skyline has changed dramatically in the last few years. Donald Trump planned on building one of his towers there though his declaration that "*In five years, Batumi will be the best city in the world!*" may have proven to be its death knell as the tower remain unrealised while the political climate is again fraught. Batoum, was probably temperate enough in December of 1919, its weather being classified as humid sub-tropical. The troops on The *Huntscastle* would soon be a lot colder.

*"We left Batoum at 1pm on Friday 12th Dec. 1919 and arrived at Novorossisk at 12 noon on Sat. 13th Dec. 1919. On entering the harbour we saw about fifteen sunken ships which the Bolshies sunk before they retreated inland. "*

## Fifteen Sunken Ships

The tale of the sunken destroyers was connected to the events of Russia's recent past, events which caused my granddad's journey. Vladimir Lenin, assisted by the Germans, had returned from exile in Switzerland to Russia with the intention of interrupting Russia's involvement in the Great War. In December 1917, Lenin, along with Leon Trotsky, began to negotiate peace with the Central Powers (Germany and Austria) and on March 3rd 1918 the Treaty of Brest-Litovsk was signed. The terms of the treaty were harsh, and it would play a large part in provoking the Russian Civil War.

The Black Sea Fleet, a part of the Imperial Russian Navy, had been making successful incursions against Turkey, allies of Germany, at the time of the treaty which demanded that the ships of the Black Sea Fleet be handed over to the Germans. To avoid this, the ships were moved from Sevastopol to Novorossiysk. But Novorossiysk was in the control of the White Army who had recently smashed the Red Army, so the Bolsheviks, wanting to keep the ships out of the hands of the Whites, scuttled much of the fleet there in June of that year. Records show eleven and not fifteen ships were scuttled: one Dreadnought, four Fidonisy Class destroyers, four destroyers and two Torpedo Boats. The Dreadnought, *Svobodnaya Rossiya*, was sunk by the *Kerch* as was the *Fidonisi*. It is said that the *Kerch* sunk more tonnage than any other destroyer from any country in The Great War, a lot of it being its own fleet. The *Kerch* was then sunk by her own crew. There is an account of the scuttling in part two of Alexei Tolstoy's trilogy, *The Ordeal,* which vividly captures the chaos and confusion of those days for those interested in more detail.

The sight of these ships may have seemed to those on the *Hunstcastle* to be a sign that the Bolsheviks were on the run but the ships had been sunk to buy time for the Bolsheviks to find their feet. By 1919 they had begun to coalesce into a fighting force which, though smaller than the White Army, was far more organised.

*"Our ship could not put into the quayside owing to bad weather so we lay in the harbour for nearly two days."*

For about 46 days a year between November and March, Novorossisk, usually sheltered, is subjected to north easterly winds from the Caucasus Mountains called the Bora which lasts from 1 to 3 days, making the bay unnavigable and causing a steep drop in temperature

e Quayside owing
d weather so u
y in the harbou
   nearly two day
nded in Novorossi
 11 am on Monday
c. 1919. The hills w
round Novorossisk
e infested by a l
brigands who ar
nown as the Gree
uards. When thes
reen Guards go sh
   stores they come
own into the town
ot it. We stopped

# Chapter Five: The War in South Russia

## A SitRep

To understand some of the issues feeding into the conflict, look at a map of Russia circa 1919 and imagine that all around the edges of what the Tsarists wanted to be one united country, was a frill of territories that were relatively recent additions to the notion of Russia. In the north and west were the Baltic States and the Poles and the Czechs fighting for independence. In the south there was the Ukraine, the home of Nestor Makhno's anarchic Black Army, agitating for independence. Further east, the Caucasus, the neck of land between the Black Sea and the Caspian Sea, had a mixed population that was even more tricky. When the Russians had conquered the North Caucasus in the 19th century, they planted settlers in an effort to integrate the territory - much like the plantation of people in 16th century Ireland. The Northern Caucasus was home to the Kuban Cossack, the Terek Cossacks, Karbardians (and possibly Kardashians), Chechens and the Inguichi all of whom were fighting like cats in a bag. The Don Cossacks held sway north of Novorossiysk and around the Don River which included Rostov and Taganrog where granddad would soon come within reach of the advancing Bolshevik Army. Cossacks mainly fought for the right to be left alone and differentiated themselves not only from other Cossack tribes but also from the average Russian peasant. The peasants in their turn understandably hated anyone who tried to take their land or livestock, which was pretty much everyone. Add any number of religious sects, mountainy people and refugees and it was an area to avoid.

Additionally, Russia's coastline is limited in comparison to its size and as much of that coastline is to the north along the Baltic and the Arctic, the warm water ports on the Black Sea, like Sevastopol and Novorossiysk, were, and are, extremely important. However, it was not only a key area geographically for the Russians. South of the Caucasus Mountains was Transcaucasia which included Armenia – which had most recently been 'cleansed' by the Turk - Georgia and Azerbaijan, for much of their history under the Ottomans and where there were two major oil fields, at Tbilisi and Baku, coveted by all. This area also encompassed trade routes to Asia, including India, in which the British had special interest. They were worried that the Russians would block access to India and the Far East. So, while the French had withdrawn in the Spring of 1919, the British remained. To defeat the Bolsheviks, and keep their trade routes clear, they had to back those who were fighting them: the Tsarists or White Army.

**The British in Russia**

The British had not entirely left Russia when the Great War ended which was partly why Churchill managed to muster a Mission. The Northern Forces at Archangel and Murmansk were the largest area of British operations. Other fronts included Siberia, the Eastern

Baltic, the Turkestan and Caspian Fronts as well as the Crimea. These theatres of war have received more attention because they received more press at the time because there were British men in combat in those areas. Even in more recent books that have the benefit of sources only recently come to light, the South Russia theatre gets relegated to footnotes. But the South was crucial. After the leader in the east, Kolchak, suffered losses through spring 1919, much British support would be directed to the south as the White Army was then making huge headway from there towards Moscow. In October 1919, when the White Army had reached Orel some 200 miles south of Moscow, it was assumed that victory was within their grasp but then, for a variety of reasons, the tables turned very quickly. The Black Army had attacked from the south-east and were making towards the White Army base at Taganrog, taking troops from the main sphere of action, the Don Cossacks withdrew as Denikin's lines were stretched to breaking. A re-organised Red Army ejected them from Orel and began pushing them south. Soon the whole White Army were in retreat south and Novorossiysk, where granddad is just about to land, was fast becoming the exit point for refugees fleeing both the Bolsheviks and the White Army.

## War Matériel

Most British support came in the form of the surplus equipment that was floating around after the Great War. Churchill persuaded

Prime Minister Lloyd George, who was not eager to send troops, that it would be cheaper to ship supplies to Russia than bring it home from various theatres of war. In fact it was partly the amount of military supplies - and men - in North Russia towards the end of the war that led to the British staying in Russia. The supplies were vast and in varying stages of disrepair. There was enough for 250,000 men – from uniforms, food, stationery, soap and toilet paper to poison gas shells, field guns, tanks, and aeroplanes, much of which ended up on the docks at Novorossiysk. In contrast the amount of men Britain sent to South Russia peaked in March 1920 at just under 1500 and they were all supposed to be training and support staff rather than combat troops.

Ultimately, the White Army's shoddy administration was incapable of getting supplies to where they were needed. Ships were unloaded onto the docks by Turkish prisoners and left unguarded. While men at the front starved and fought in rags, Novorossiysk contained some of the best-dressed and well-fed White Army officers around while prostitutes in the port were seen wearing nurses' uniforms and the town was a magnet for every kind of trader, bandit, and robber around.

## General Herbert Holman

Third and final head of the Mission in South Russia - June 1919- March 1920 - General Herbert Holman had a curious mix of attributes. Ambitious and intelligent, responsible for many commands and near the end of a distinguished career he was still somehow unjaded, almost boy-like, and alive to the human suffering around him. A few photographs show him running about or talking to Russian children as if he was unable to keep still. He was seemingly not weighed down by the war, rather determined to do something about it. Holman would play a small part in my granddad's survival.

There is little biographical information on Holman. He had qualified as an interpreter in both French and Russian, had been to Sandhurst, served in Burma and India, was a staff officer during the Boxer rebellion in China, worked in intelligence at Whitehall in London for a number of years, served with the Russian army in Manchuria during the Russo-Japanese War and with the Indian Army, intelligence branch, from 1914. After Russia he would return to India until his retirement in 1928.

FIG.11. GENERAL HERBERT HOLMAN, JULY 1919. PHOTOGRAPHER UNKNOWN. SOURCE: IWM

Unlike those officers of the Great War, he was addicted to being at the front and he liked to fly with the RAF to get a good view of the state of play.

A crash landing at Ekaterinodar on January the 11<sup>th</sup> 1920 in time to address the soldiers there seems to be nothing out of the ordinary for him. One gets an image of the plane careering to the ground and Holman striding from the wreckage without a moustache hair out of place. A Captain Lever, Senior Wireless Office at Taganrog said...

*'Twould be better if the General stayed occasionally at the base and made some attempt at running the show instead of spending the whole of his time sculling about in an aeroplane at the front doing spectacular stunts in the way of bomb dropping. Most of us have never had a glimpse of the man.'*

During the evacuation of Novorossiysk Lieutenant Colonel Lister would note...

*'He will not speak seriously on the subject of retirement [retreat]. His usual reply if you mention such unpleasant facts is "Let's take an aeroplane and tank and bomb the blighters.'*

Some would blame his absence from base in December 1919 - when he was tearing around in trains rescuing people - for the chaotic retreat at Taganrog which granddad would be a part of. Lieutenant Colonel Lister wrote...

*I gather his [Holman's]' presence at Taganrog might have made all the difference in our getting our aeroplanes and ordnance stores away. I don't think he appreciates the seriousness of the situation'.*

The Russians appreciated Holman even if some of his men did not. He was made an honorary Cossack by one Don and two Kuban Cossack stanitsas in 1919. The Don Cossacks would fight hard along the Whites for their homelands north of the Kuban district in which Novorossiysk was situated but the Kuban Cossacks were not as pugnacious, and their morale was bad and though Holman signed proclamations urging them to fight and had those proclamations air dropped over their territory - in fact probably flew those drops himself - they would not be roused. The Kuban's lack of will contributed to the collapse of the White retreat and thus to the chaos at Novorossiysk. Holman would play a small part in my granddad's story, both his near abandonment of the last of the Mission and their rescue.

## The Volunteer Army and The White Army

From August 26, 1918 until March 27, 1920, Novorossiysk was the one of the principal centres of General Anton Denikin's White Army, sometimes known as The Volunteer Army from which it developed. Initially the Volunteer Army consisted of actual volunteers eager to restore a United Russia. It was conservative and consisted of military officers, cadets, university students and even secondary school students, but once a system of payment was put in place and conscription and drafting began, ranks swelled to include a host of people with diverse motives, foremost of which, in the south at least, was independence, quite the opposite of the United Russia ideal beloved of The Volunteers. Soon the term White was being used. In Lauri Kopistos' *The British Intervention in South Russia 1918-1920* he explains the use of the term White…

*'White' (belye) is used to describe the various conservative, officer-dominated anti-Bolshevik armies of the Civil War, such as the Volunteer Army of South Russia, Kolchak's Siberian Army and Iudenich's North-western Army. This term was first used by the Bolsheviks to discredit their opponents referring to the standard of the Bourbons and the French monarchists. It was however soon accepted by these anti-Bolsheviks themselves, and also the Allies used it.* But the Volunteer Army remained a force in themselves, and they were the main thrust of the attempt on Moscow.

The White Army and their Cossack allies remained stuck in old ways of warfare, throwing great numbers into the fray to slog it out. This depended very much on cavalry. This was a continual frustration to the British who, along with other nations, had made huge advances in staging modern warfare during the Great War. The atmosphere of the Russian Civil War was described by one officer as 'Napoleonic'. This refusal by the conservative Volunteer and White Army to learn compared with the Bolsheviks forward looking, radical thinking, would contribute to their downfall.

## General Anton Denikin

If the British were going to send stuff to Russia, they needed to have one person who would represent the cacophony of interests there. They favoured dealing with General Anton Ivanovich Denikin. Denikin had come from humble beginnings and had progressed to being a Lieutenant General in the Imperial Russian Army during the Great War. He supported an attempted coup in 1917, was imprisoned but escaped with General Kornilov and fled to the Don territory in the Northern Caucasus in the winter of 1917-18 where they formed the anti-Bolshevik Volunteer Army with General Alekseev. While General Kolchak in the east was the Head of State and as such oversaw the

FIG.12. GENERAL ANTON DENIKIN C. 1918, PHOTO: UNKNOWN. SOURCE PUBLICATION: THE TIMES HISTORY OF THE WAR. LONDON: THE TIMES, P. 399.

whole show and had also been receiving supplies from Britain, once he was routed in the Urals (ouch) in the first half of 1919, Denikin became head of the White resistance and the chief receiver of British supplies. Churchill favoured Denikin and the second head of the British Mission, General Sir Charles Briggs, described Denikin as a 'strong, clear-headed and determined man', but others had their doubts. While he was recognised for his meteoric rise, his patriotism and some great successes in 1919, he was a bad administrator. When Denikin was asked for an estimate of his forces so the British could supply them, he wildly over-estimated his numbers leading to huge waste. Denikin's officers were widely seen as being lazy and arrogant. They were aristocrats and monarchists who enjoyed the comfortable life at headquarters instead of being at the front with their men. General Wrangel, one of the more honourable White generals, who would eventually receive the poisoned cup of command, once admired Denikin but Denikin's refusal to listen to any advice, his continual undermining of Wrangel and his increasingly muddled and contradictory orders would destroy their relationship, while his insistence on a united Russia would divide the Volunteer Army, and contribute to their downfall. Meanwhile, the British on the ground would find out that Denikin's Army was just as brutal as the Red Army. He was a known anti-Semite and Denikin's Volunteers are said to have been responsible for several pogroms against the Jewish people.

## The Cossacks

The Cossacks influenced the outcomes of several battles, both positively and negatively. We in the west know of Cossacks as men who wear big furry hats, drink vodka all day long and perform athletic squat dances around campfires and all of that is true to some extent, including the squat dance which makes up part of a Ukrainian folk dance. They were also excellent horsemen, warriors and fiercely independent in spirit. The word Cossack comes from Kazak which means adventurer or free man. Most sources say the Cossack hosts, which originated around the Black and Caspian Seas, were made up of peasants fleeing serfdom in the 16th and 17th centuries along with other refugees, mavericks and mercenaries that found themselves adrift on the Asian steppes in response to one political shift or another. The blood of the Cossacks ran thick with the spirit of independence, and they would trade on their military might, fighting for various Tsars and others, in return for permission to rule themselves. If you were a Cossack or accepted into one Cossack host or another you abandoned your nationality. You were no longer a Russian, Pole, German or a Turk, you were a Cossack. They fought alongside the Whites in the hope of retaining their independence after the war and were very much not fighting to be part of a larger whole. There were a number of Cossack hosts, mainly in the south of Russia and their determined independence would have contributed to the fall of the

Whites. The Kuban Cossacks would falter between backing the Ukrainian Independence fighters of the area and fighting to retain their autonomy and Kuban Cossack politicians would break with Denikin. The Don Cossack was the largest host, numbering around 1.5 million before the war, and it was the Don who fought the hardest alongside the Whites - though they withdrew their support at a crucial point at Orel - and the Don who lost the most. The Soviet victory would result in the decossackization of the Steppe and the dissolution of a once great war force. General Pytor Wrangel led a Cossack Division during The Great War and in the last stages of the civil war became a representative of four separate Cossacks groups - The Don, Terek, Kuban and Astrakhan - an unprecedented alliance in the face of the Bolsheviks.

## The Dashing General Pytor Wrangel

General Wrangel is one of the more obvious heroes of the era. A man of principle, he cuts a strikingly elegant figure in the photographs of him. Born in what would become Lithuania, to a Baltic-German noble family in 1878, he would graduate in mining engineering from Rostov Technical School and receive his first army commission in 1902. During the First World War he commanded a cavalry corp. He became disillusioned with the nepotism of the Russian Army, but he remained close to the Tsar and at the opening of the Civil War he joined the White Army. He would lead the army - comprising mainly of Kuban Cossacks - that took Tsaritsyn in July 1919. Wrangel had not approved of Denikin's rapid advance on Moscow in the late summer of 1919 and disapproved of the state of the undisciplined army, something which was also frustrating the British. Wrangel believed Denikin was over-extending his lines. He had a point, but perhaps Denikin had little choice but

FIG.13 THE DASHING GENERAL PYTOR WRANGEL IN SEVASTOPOL, APRIL 1920. PHOTOGRAPHER UNKNOWN. SOURCE WWW.EN.TOPWAR.RU, 2004.

to act fast and bank on victory before the White Army disintegrated or the Reds grew too strong.

Wrangel was dismissed or resigned from the army - depending on which account you believe - in January of 1920 after protracted disagreements with Denikin, whose evasive and contradictory manner and orders as well as a refusal to listen to his generals made it impossible for Wrangel to continue. He would be recalled to head the remnants of the White resistance in the Crimea from March to November 1920. Perhaps Wrangel's honour contributed to the White downfall as, if he had ignored the chain of command and seized power, the outcome could have been different.

After the Civil War, Wrangel and his wife Olga settled in Brussels. He would be an organiser and leader of the Russians in exile and as such was a thorn in the side of the Soviet regime. He published his memoirs – *Always with Honour* - in 1928 before he died suddenly. It is said he was poisoned by his butler's brother who may have been a Soviet agent, something that became a bit of a tradition for the Soviets. General Wrangel's wife Olga went to live in New York where she became lifelong friends with General Denikin's wife. General Wrangel's son Alexis would move to Ireland where he died in 2005. His funeral service was held only 20 miles way from Clonaslee in Co. Offaly where my granddad had been posted during the 1930s and where his daughter Mary, who died aged 8 from mushroom poisoning, was buried. The honourable Wrangel, along with General Holman, would play a part in my granddad's survival, not that they or my granddad ever knew.

## The Red Army

I'll keep it ludicrously brief considering their role in history but there is plenty about them elsewhere. The Red Army of Bolsheviks were radical revolutionaries and with their beliefs, their rapidly swelling numbers and the leadership of Trotsky, though new to war, they were a more than able force. They were responsible for the Red Terror which saw the execution Between 1918 and 1922 of 100,000 (Lincoln, 1989, p.384) or more of many of their enemies. While this terror loomed large in the imaginations of those in the west, The Whites were quite as savage. The Red Army was he most successful of a global movement towards better workers' rights. Back in Ireland there were several short-lived Soviets (communist councils) during these years including one in Limerick and one in Waterford at the gas works which seceded from the state and raised the red flag on the Waterside in 1923 for nearly three months.

## The Green Army

The Green Army or Green Guards, were comprised mostly of landed peasants and was a loose-knit coalition that came together to resist the Soviets. The group was particularly enraged by the communist's policy of confiscating crop harvests and livestock to feed the urban poor and the Red Army. Starting in 1917, they waged a five-year struggle against the Bolsheviks in which they ambushed, harassed and sometimes even massacred whole Red Army units, in addition to liberating towns from Moscow's grip and sabotaging Soviet infrastructure. The faction armed itself with weapons gathered from defeated opponents. Its rank eventually swelled with deserting Red and White army troops and the urban poor in addition to peasants. Some Green army brigades numbered as high as 50,000, while smaller cells were only a few hundred strong. Ultimately the movement, which was little more than a loose federation, lacked an overall political strategy or a vision for the future. The Bolsheviks painted the Greens as reactionaries and class enemies and often characterized them as being in league with the Whites. By 1922, the Greens petered out as the Soviets strengthened their grip. We will be seeing more of the Greens.

**The Black and Blue Armies**

The Independent Army of the Ukraine or The Black Army, led by the charismatic Nestor Makhno, were also called Makhnovists after their leader. They were Anarchists operating in and around the Crimean Peninsula just east of where granddad was. The Anarchists were quite organised, they had some military success, but they were trying to fight off the Reds and the Whites and up an anarchist state in southeastern Ukraine all at the same time.

They have little to do with our story apart from some knock-on effects from their activities. The Blues were like the Greens in that they fought the soviets, but they were more organised. As they were based near Moscow they were brutally put down and they don't come into our story. I mostly just added them for the 'Black & Blue' section title because in the end everyone came out black and blue. Imagine the Wild West with bigger guns, worse weather, more factions, lots of soap, better stationery, and only one railway line. Throw in a princess or two, some disgruntled Turks and Cossacks and you are probably getting close to the reality of it. It was into this chaos granddad's unit would land, soon afterwards to head north into the maw of the advancing Red Army to assist in the retreat. We rejoin him on the train north.

FIG.14. BLACK ARMY LEADER, NESTOR MAKHNO, IN A HOLDING CAMP, ROUMANIA, C.1921.

up in Novorossisk
we went up to
We entrained
tle trucks en-rou
Taganrog via
katerinodar & Rosto
6 pm. on Thursday
c. 1919. We arrived
ostov at 2 pm on S
1st Dec. 1919. We arr
Taganrog at 3 a
Monday 22nd Dec.
stopped on the tr
ntil daylight. We
rrived at the Miss
eadquarters at 11 a

# Chapter Six: Up the Line

## Railway War

*"We stopped two days in Novorossisk & then we went up the line. We en-trained in cattle trucks en-route for Taganrog via Ekaterinodar & Rostov at 6pm on Thursday 18th Dec. 1919."*

Taganrog would be the furthest thrust of granddad's journey though it is far from over. He was heading into a dangerous and chaotic situation and in a cattle truck no less. The line my granddad travelled up was the same for everyone: Novorossiysk - Ekaterinodar (now Krasnodar)-Rostov-Taganrog. The reason for this is that though South Russia was vast, there were few usable roads and the best way to get anywhere was by train. Armoured trains were used by both sides as artillery support and as mobile command centres. Infantry and others followed in peasant carts. The White Army had made huge advances in 1919, getting to within 200 miles of Moscow, but, as the advance was made along the railway, the ground they gained only extended out as far as the cavalry ranged, about 15 miles on each flank. Beyond that narrow corridor, soldiers, bandits, peasants, and revolutionaries from all sides travelled relatively freely. While the railway meant the advance was fast, it was one of the main reasons for the White Army's collapse after a seemingly successful 1919: their supply lines were long and over-extended. The retreat would prove to be just as fast.

## British Military Winter Kit: South Russia

As they headed up the line they also travelling into winter. At the back of his account my granddad included a list of his Winter Kit. Most items are self-explanatory. The housewife was not a lady but a roll with a sewing kit in it. The housewife would be inside a holdall. Nowadays a holdall as a bag with handles but in this case, it is a roll of fabric with pouches for various items. A button brush was used to polish their buttons and the button stick was used to keep the Brasso off the material of the uniform. Webbing is strips of tough fabric. You will find rucksacks, satchels and belts made from it both in army surplus stores and dangling from students. The British Army replaced leather equipment with webbing equipment after the Boer War but with the outbreak of the Great War, because demand was so great, some leather equipment was still also used. Webbing equipment is now called *Personal Load Carrying Equipment*. As for the fur hat and overcoat, I do not know if granddad had them and they certainly didn't find their way back if he did. It is likely that, pragmatic as ever, if he did bring them back, he sold or swapped them.

## Articles of kit we had in Russia.

### Ordinary English kit.

| | |
|---|---|
| 3 shirts | 1 knife. |
| 2 undervests | 1 fork |
| 3 prs socks | 1 spoon |
| 2 " underpants | 1 button brush |
| 2 " boots | 1 shaving " |
| 1 pr. breeches | 1 tooth " |
| 1 " trousers | 1 hair " |
| 1 pr. putties | 2 boot brushes |
| 2 tunics | 1 comb |
| 1 cap | 1 button stick |
| 1 overcoat | 1 housewife |
| 1 cardigan | 1 holdall |
| 2 towels | 1 pr braces |

— P.T.O.

Articles of kit we had in Russia

### Ordinary English Kit. Cont'd.

| | |
|---|---|
| 1 jack knife | 2 suits overalls |
| 1 lanyard | 1 tin of Dublin |

### Russian Winter Kit.

| | |
|---|---|
| 1 flying helmet or fur cap | 1 pr. field boots |
| | 1 " sea boots |
| 1 fur overcoat | 1 " woollen gloves |
| 1 leather jerkin | 1 " fingerless " |
| 2 cap comforters | 4 blankets |
| 1 woollen muffler | 2 prs of long woollen stockings |
| 1 pr. snow glasses | |
| 1 field dressing | 2 extra prs. socks. |

P.T.O.

## Articles of kit we had in Russia.

### Russian Summer Kit.

| | |
|---|---|
| 2 prs. Khaki drill trousers or shorts. | 1 Sun helmet |
| 2 Khaki drill tunics | 1 Spine protector. |
| | 1 Mosquito net. |

### Arms & Ammunition.

| | |
|---|---|
| 1 rifle | 150 rounds of rifle ammunition |
| 1 revolver | |
| 1 bayonet | 100 rounds of revolver ammunition |
| 1 revolver holster | |
| 1 revolver cleaning rod | 1 rifle pull through |
| 1 rifle cleaning brush | 1 oil bottle. |

1 complete set of webbing equipment.

*"When we were in Taganrog we saw some old cannon balls buried in the walls of the hospital which were used by our fleet in the bombardment of Taganrog during the Crimea War."*

Taganrog was the centre of operations for the White Army and the British Mission. The British Tank Corps training base had been there from May 1919 and though they had limited success in training the Russians, the tanks would be used to good effect during the retreat as just the sight of them scared the Red Army. Granddad was with the RAF who were now also based at Taganrog.

**The RAF in South Russia**

The RAF (previously the RFC or Royal Flying Corps) arrived in South Russia in the summer of 1919 in the form of the 47th Squadron. While granddad was not involved in the squadrons nor did he fly, he would end up burning some of their planes. But the RAF's movements and escapades, both in the air and on the ground, provide an overview, sometimes literally, of what was a violent and complicated time.

In charge of RAF Training Mission was Lieutenant Colonel Arthur Maund. Maund seems to have been something of a bureaucrat. John T. Smith recounts in his book *Gone to Russia to Fight* how Maund sent a letter to Commanding Officer of 47th Squadron Canadian ace Raymond Collishaw criticising his record keeping regarding a Ford van he and some other pilots had "requisitioned" earlier that year. The letter was written as the Bolsheviks moved in. Raymond Collishaw was one of the greatest fighter pilots of all time with little time for paperwork. He was handsome and had the sort of gung-ho attitude that would become part and parcel of the fighter pilot myth. Another pilot tells of a time Collishaw was a passenger in a plane that crashed in the desert. Disentangling himself from the wreckage Collishaw said...

*"If only we had some beer, we could have a party."*

FIG. 15. AIR ACE, RAYMOND COLLISHAW

Later he would write of his time in Russia that it was the first campaign he had conducted *'totally without whisky. But not without vodka.'* Collishaw's 47th squadron consisted of Flights A, B, C and Z (Z Flight was a secret unit created in late 1919 by The British Mission HQ at Taganrog with the aim of bombing Moscow, a mission which would never get off the ground - so to speak. The 47th was based at Taganrog for the period granddad was there though they used train carriages as mobile bases up and down the line.

Each RAF flight unit had their own armoured train, a mobile base complete with sleeping quarters, messes, workshops, and supplies. The procedure was for the senior pilot to fly down the track looking for an area beside the track which was suitable as a landing strip. The pilot would land and wait for the train which could take hours or days. When the train with the mobile base arrived, the Flight could commence flying missions.

The RAF in Russia flew DH9s primarily but there were also 130 RE8's and B Flight would fly Sopwith Camels from September 1919. Their job was to train Russian pilots but as time was short often a pilot would get only a few hours flying time. This resulted so many crashes of RE8s that the Russians began to believe the RE8s were faulty planes that had already been rejected by the British. Training the Russians was frustrating for the RAF as it was for the tank and artillery units. Captain Hugh Boustead, a Lewis gun instructor said of the Russians:

'Training the soldiers was delightful since they were so gentle and straightforward, and at the same time maddening because they were forgetful and lazy. Their interest was intense for a short time, and then quite suddenly they would say to themselves, 'I know it all now,' and *nothing but firm driving or bitter experience at the front would make them learn more'*

(Wright, 2017, p.401-402)

It is little wonder there were planes dropping out of the sky. It is for this reason that British soldiers often found themselves fighting in the Civil War. Additionally, the 47th Squadron, sent to Russia from Salonika, were a fighting unit rather than a training one and many air aces had volunteered. It was inevitable that the British would take to the skies. The pilots flew many bombing missions, including up the Volga and in the Ukraine and proved indispensable to the White Army, especially to General Wrangel in the taking of Tsaritsyn - later renamed Stalingrad- in June 1919. They also provided accounts of how it was on the ground. B Flight would enter Tsaritsyn after its fall. Marion Aten of B-Flight wrote...

*In every street bodies, animal and human, lay rotting...in the rubbled street with their shattered houses our whispers came back to us in hollow echoes. People staggered through doorways into the sun and sat witlessly picking at their rags of clothes. Starving children looked at us blankly. In such a place in seemed sacrilege to be alive.* (Aten, 1961, p.76)

Some of the adventures of 47th Squadron capture the precarious and freewheeling spirit of flying in the early days of aviation. In the summer of 1919, two DH9s took off on a reconnaissance mission.

Because of the heat, the crews, a captain and observer in each craft, were dressed only in shorts and shirts. One of the planes sustained ground fire which holed its fuel tank. The observer, a Lieutenant Mitchell, climbed out onto the wing and plugged the leak with his thumb. The second plane was forced to land at which point a unit of Bolshevik cavalry bore down on them. The first plane, with the holed fuel tank, held off the cavalry, then landed where Mitchell continued to fire at the horsemen while the crew of the second plane torched their craft and scrambled into Mitchells' cockpit on the first plane, which took off, Mitchell resuming his place on the wing. The flight back to base took 50 minutes. Mitchells' legs were burned from exhaust gases. Both he and his captain were awarded DSO's (Distinguished Service Orders).

At home in Britain, the more involved the RAF became, the less enthusiastic the British public became about being part of the offensive. When in October 1919 the RAF was officially made part of the non-combatant British Military Mission, the men of the flight squadrons worked around their non-combatant status by volunteering for missions. They would continue to fly until the final evacuation in March 1920.

### 'The Bolshies are steadily advancing'

*"We arrived at Taganrog at 3am on Monday 22nd Dec. 1919 & stopped on the train until daylight. We arrived at the Mission Headquarters at 11am on the same date. When we*

*arrived at Taganrog the Sea of Azov which was facing our depot was frozen."*

The White retreat had begun as far back as late October 1919 with the defeat at Orel. By Christmas when granddad's unit was moving north, the retreat south was a rout. Everyone fleeing the Red Army travelled along the railway line which turned into a bottleneck at Rostov with Novorossiysk at its mouth. Typically, my granddad says nothing about conditions in the cattle truck travelling for days over the frozen steppe. While trains carrying army and refugees were travelling south, the RAF mobile units moved up and down the line and the British Military Mission men, including my granddad, moved north. Doubtless there were junctions and side-lines, but the limited means of escape would contribute hugely to a sense of anxiety especially in wintertime when other modes of travel on the southern steppe would have been impossible. Red Saboteurs were rife up and down the line too. One night an aircraft man from B Flight called Carstairs caught and killed a Bolshevik saboteur setting explosives on one of the carriages. With the freezing weather - in which many froze to death - the protracted travel times, the presumable lack of sleep, the probably primitive toilet arrangements, and the threat of typhus, which was spreading like wildfire through the retreating hordes, as well as the saboteurs and bandits, it was probably close to hellish.

In the summer of 1919, Taganrog had been a pleasant posting, the area being safely under the command of the White Army. For the soldiers, activities like sailing, going to the cinema and concerts were usual. By December the previous, idyllic summer was a fading memory, temperatures had plunged, and the Red Army were closing in. Granddad had arrived in time to retreat.

*"On Christmas Eve we went into town and had a look round. It is only a small town. We had a good dinner. On Boxing Day we made preparations for a retreat."*

General Denikin and his officers had a lavish Christmas dinner at Taganrog only days before the evacuation. According to Lauri Kopisto's 2011 dissertation, the British only found out that the Whites were leaving, and the Bolsheviks close to the city, from their own artillery instructors at the last minute. Three different sources say that the Bolsheviks were in Taganrog by the 24th or 25th of December and this includes tales of a gun fight in the railway yards in Marion Aten's *Last Train Over Rostov Bridge* but granddad writes that he left on New Year's Day, and surely even he could not be that insouciant surrounded by Bolsheviks? He does say…

*"There was a good deal of anxiety in the depot in case the Bolshies would take Rostov & then we would be completely cut off."*

Due to Taganrog being west of Rostov the threat of being cut off from Novorossiysk was very real.

*"On Sat. 27th Dec. 1919 we had a wireless message saying- 'The Bolshies are still steadily advancing".*

This message was probably from British artillery instructors who were at the front. Captain Frecheville, aged 24, and Lieutenant H.J. Couche were machine gun instructors who had been ordered to the outer defences of Rostov and captured when the Bolsheviks attacked after receiving no resistance from the White Army, which, presumably, had fled. Kopisto dates their capture as being in December 1919, whereas Wright's book, puts it as January 9th 1920 which makes more sense as Rostov had just fallen on that day.

But the fate of the artillery instructors was not learned until late January 1920 when it was discovered that the Bolsheviks stripped them, beat them to death with sticks and had their bodies dragged behind horses through the streets of Rostov.

FIG. 16. CAPTAIN WILLIAM FRECHEVILLE OF THE ROYAL ENGINEERS ONE OF THE FEW BRITISH SOLDIERS KILLED BY THE RED ARMY. SOURCE: WWW.EWHURSTFALLEN.CO.UK. 2005.

## Death on the Steppe

So, the 'Bolshies' were coming bringing terror and death, there were bodies everywhere but, for the British, there was still time for a funeral.

*"We had a military funeral on the same date (27th) & I was one of the coffin bearers. The man we buried died of typhus."*

The official count of British casualties during the Intervention was 4 dead, 10 wounded and 5 missing (later declared dead) but the Haidar Pasha Memorial at Istanbul lists 41 dead - 23 from the RAF and 18 from the Navy - as those who died from illness were included in the total. The best candidate for the funeral granddad attended was Frank Oliver Freeman, a general clerk with 47 squadron's A Flight commanded by Raymond Collishaw. He fell ill in Krinichnaya, now Krynychna, 160 km north of Taganrog where A Flight stayed through Christmas and Boxing Day. The RAF's A Flight's retreat was re-directed away from Taganrog to the Crimea, purportedly by an anti-British White Russian Officer, a Captain Zamarev, later court-martialled, who claimed the railway to Rostov was closed. This happened close to the date my granddad was pallbearer, so maybe Freeman was prepared for burial there, placed in a coffin, and his body taken to Sevastopol. Or else he is buried in Taganrog, except not officially. He was twenty, the same age as granddad. He was the son of John and

Agnes Freeman of 8 Middle Row, Chipping Norton. His father was a Hairdresser, Tobacconist & Umbrella Maker.

Holman would step in and force the way to Rostov open again for the last of the Mission to leave but too late for A Flight's train already heading for the Crimea on a journey plagued with Bolshevik saboteurs breaking up the lines. Sometimes, in cartoon-like fashion, they would have to rip up track they had just passed to replace missing areas ahead. The typhus that had killed the soldier in the coffin granddad carried was rife. Pilot Raymond Collishaw had contracted it and nearly died surviving only due to the ministrations of a sympathetic Russian. A Flight would transport as many civilians as they could to Sevastopol in The Crimea and Collishaw ordered all dead bodies be thrown off the train to try and prevent the spread of disease, but many refugees hid the bodies of their children, and the disease, spread by lice, continued to spread rapidly.

*"We had an order come through saying-pack up all stores if possible & be ready to retreat within six hours. We worked hard at packing up stores until 2am on New Year's Day. Before starting to retreat we exploded all our bombs, burned some aeroplanes & the petrol dump & also destroyed the wireless installation."*

It is probable that it was newly refurbished Sopwith Camels that my granddad burned. These small planes, introduced in 1917, shot down more enemy craft in World War One than any other Allied plane. Unfortunately, they were also known to kill just as many of their pilots. The British would take as much as they could with them, but the list of supplies left behind occupied four pages of General Holman's' final report.

ard 4 on the ma
the station durin
ich we were up
knees in snow
mandeered all sl
orse traffic at th
ayonet point. Wh
got to Taganrog
tion which was
mile walk, we
commandeer a tro
left Taganrog a
m on Friday 2nd
20. The distance fr
aganrog to Rostov
bout sixty mile

# Chapter Seven: Retreat

## Leaving Taganrog

*"We started retreating at 3pm on New Years Day and we took all our Bolshie prisoners with us. I was one of the advance guard and on the march to the station during which we were up to our knees in snow we commandeered all sleigh and horse traffic at the bayonet point."*

The retreat proper began. This entry in granddad's account contains the first and last mention of Bolshevik prisoners. The British were officially not meant to be involved in the war and this no doubt included not taking prisoners but the reality in a chaotic situation was different. Taking prisoners may have been unavoidable. Both the Whites and the Reds had little compunction executing their enemies and to hand them over to the White forces would have amounted to the same as execution. No other account mentions prisoners at this point.

There was at least 5km between British HQ and Taganrog train station through the snow in the bitter cold and dark with another 450km via Rostov to cover to get to safety at Novorossiysk. The British were often regarded as national heroes in White held cities, but rural areas were less enthusiastic and often even ignorant of the intervention. As refugees from all points north continued to pour through the area trying to reach Novorossiysk, friendly responses would not have been guaranteed. Commandeering sleighs can't have made them any more popular. The difficulties of evacuation were exacerbated by the Russian with their propensity for looting and running away, usually both at once. General Wrangel tried to staunch the flow of deserters and loot by appointing bands of soldiers to search trains, seize stolen objects, send deserters back to the front and shoot marauders but he was fighting a losing battle.

*'The war is becoming to some a means to grow rich; re-equipment has degenerated into pillage and peculation.'*     *(*Wrangel, p.91.)

During the retreat south the Whites, including Commander-in-Chief Denikin, would abandon troops, civilians and British liaison people to fend for themselves. It was common for White Army officers to commandeer trains to bring their loot from the front lines, leaving people stranded. A string of railway cars containing tanks and artillery were abandoned at Taganrog station when an engine 'disappeared', probably to haul some general's swag. When the time came for the Whites to leave Taganrog, departing Russian Generals refused to take anyone other than British officers on their train, an unusual act of generosity given their record of taking no-one at all. Many would end up walking at least part of the way. Swarms of civilian refugees heading south would be left largely in the hands of the British.

*"The rolling-stock belonging to the troops has taken on enormous dimensions - some regiments have two hundred carriages in their wake. A considerable number of troops have retreated to the interior, and many officers are away on prolonged missions, busy selling and exchanging loot. The Army is absolutely demoralized and is fast becoming a collection of tradesmen and profiteers. All those employed on re-equipment work - that is to say, nearly all the officers - have enormous sums of money in their possession; as a result, there has been an outbreak of debauchery, gambling and wild orgies."* (Wrangel, 1928, p.91.)

While Taganrog was in danger, it was Rostov-on-Don 70km to the east that was the bottleneck everyone would have to pass through. Though A Flight would get through to Sevastopol, by the time of my granddad's retreat the Bolsheviks had gained total control in the area leaving Novorossiysk as the only possible escape route. When they reached Taganrog station, still the same building today as it was then, there were no trains available.

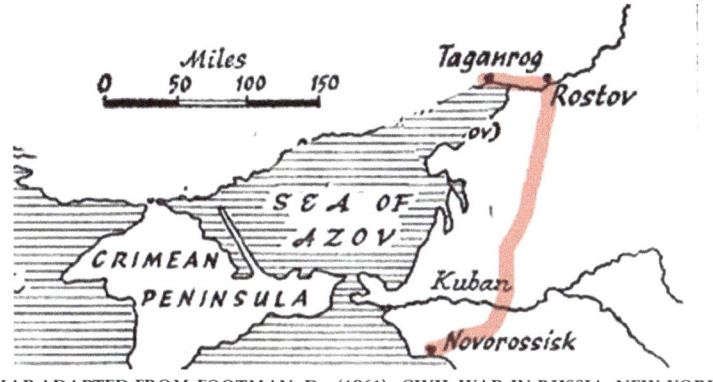

MAP ADAPTED FROM FOOTMAN, D., (1961), CIVIL WAR IN RUSSIA, NEW YORK: FREDRICK A., PRAEGER.

*"When we got to Taganrog station which was a four mile walk, we had to commandeer a train."*

## Last Train Over Rostov Bridge

January 1st, New Year's Day evening, at Taganrog. Granddad has arrived at the train station with others of the Military Mission to find there are no trains to Rostov, so they commandeer one. Whose train is it though? Where did it come from?

There are various accounts of the retreat, the most famous being Marion Aten's book, *Last Train over Rostov Bridge*. Published in 1961 while the Iron Curtain was still very much in place, it was one of the few accounts of this forgotten mission and it quickly became the main source for the period. While it was, and remains, a gripping read that recreates what the situation must have been like, it was later understood to mix in some passages of fiction with fact and is now taken with a pinch of salt. However much of the information (barring an unfortunate love story) fits in with historical fact. Aten was with B Flight who were in the same area moving the same direction as granddad. But, if I take granddad's account to be correct, then B Flight were a considerable way ahead of the last men out of Taganrog.

In Aten's account, the Whites were retreating around the 21st or 22nd of December (I dated this episode by working backwards and forwards from Christmas Eve and New Years' Eve in Aten's account), which seems to be about right as they left before the British were aware they were leaving. But, as mentioned, Aten also records a shootout with the red army in Taganrog train yards on around December 19$^{th}$ *before* granddad arrived there, saying they kept the reds from advancing to the town. This I suppose is possible.

Aten says B Flight's train was overtaken by the last one from Taganrog HQ on around December 23rd carrying Lieutenant Colonel Arthur Maund (at that point Acting Brigadier-General), head of the RAF training mission. This was the day *after* granddad had *arrived* at Taganrog. Aten also writes that this train had been given to Maund and the Mission by General Wrangel who had returned to Taganrog to find his army had abandoned the British (Aten, p.208). But Wrangel records he promised to send a train from Rostov for the last of the British at Taganrog on January 1$^{st}$ (Wrangel dates his order as December 19th however the Whites were still using the Julian calendar, Wrangel, p.97). Wrangel, moving quickly to try and bring order to the retreat, would be in Rostov around January 1$^{st}$ and 2$^{nd}$ with General Holman.

According to Aten, B Flight's train caught up with Maund's train broken down some miles out of Rostov on December 26th when granddad and his pals were only beginning preparation for retreat at Taganrog. Maund came to their train to reassure the men he was not going to steal their engine. Shortly after he left, their engine is heard to move off, leaving B Flight stranded. Raymond Collishaw, writing in the 1960s seems to back up Aten's account of Maund's treachery, though Collishaw was with A Flight heading to The Crimea at that point. Maund's account as recounted in Julian Lewis's *Racing Ace...* (Chapter 5) differs in that he claims B Flight's train had broken down and that when he reached Rostov, he sent his men onto Novorossiysk while he stayed behind to try and save B Flight's train. B Flight would be brought to Rostov yards by another engine, arriving there on New Year's Eve when granddad and the boys were exploding aeroplanes back in Taganrog. B Flight would have to walk over Rostov Bridge to escape, probably around January 9th (according to Maund) but perhaps earlier.

In the revised edition of *Last Train Over Rostov Bridge* (2011), Major George Treloar, who was also one of the last out of Taganrog writes that Wrangel sent two trains ten hours apart from Rostov for the abandoned British and that Wrangel had mostly taken over the running of the trains between Taganrog and Rostov. Treloar also notes other mistakes in Aten's account, notably the whereabouts of A Flight and that Maund was not on the last train out of Taganrog as Aten claims because he, Treloar, was himself, left behind at Taganrog with 100 Mission men and they did not get out until early in the New Year, which matches granddad's account. My feeling is Aten (or Arthur Orrmont with whom he wrote the book) inserted a few days or even a week into his account to make way for a fictional love story. Indeed John T. Smith in *Gone to Russia to Fight* places B Flight in Taganrog on January 1st (Chapter 17). Smith also says Holman and another officer went in search of some missing Mission evacuees.

As far as I can make out then, granddad got on a train at Taganrog after B Flight had passed through to Rostov. The train, unknown to him, had been organised by General Wrangel. Colonel Treloar may also have been on that train though there is the possibility, given granddad's account, that he was part of a small crew left behind to destroy stores and look after prisoners. Either way he was on the last or one of the last trains over Rostov bridge. He was certainly on the last one out of Taganrog. The speed of his arrival and departure at Rostov seems to back this up. I credit Wrangel, and possibly Holman, who was zipping about on trains rescuing people, with saving granddad's skin and by extension, my own.

*"We left Taganrog at 5am on Friday 2nd Jan. 1920. The distance from Taganrog to Rostov is about sixty miles but it took us three and a half days to get there."*

Taganrog fell on January 4th. Granddad's journey to Rostov began on January 2nd and took until January 6th. He typically says nothing of the journey, but Aten's book, muddied dates aside, provides something academic work does not: the feel and the smell of actual participation in human struggle and tragedy.

*The trip to Rostov was another exercise in Jobian patience. The line crept forward, a mile an hour, sometimes only two or three miles in a morning, an afternoon. When we passed a station, it was necessary to keep our engine jammed tight against the rear of the train ahead; otherwise, refugee coaches, waiting for a box-car length of space to pounce on, would cut in line. Seaward, three hundred yards at this point, lay the Azov, cold and bleak and fog shrouded. The wagon road on the landward side of the tracks was black with refugees, soldiers and mounted Cossacks on patrol. The civilians and military travelled in carts, sleighs, on horse and on foot. Both were typhus-ridden, and bodies, some stripped of their outer clothing, dotted the landscape.*

*On our third day out the staff cars began passing on the open track. Drawn-faced officers stood looking dully out of the windows of coaches clicking by at express train speed. Obviously, Taganrog was being evacuated. One string of trains had palatial dining cars in which an orchestra and jugglers entertained a fat general with white, close-cropped hair. In cinema dramas to come of the Civil War, I thought, such a scene would undoubtedly figure.*

*The misery I had seen aboard the trains, heart-rending though it was nothing compared to that of the road. Singly and together scores of refugees lay dying and dead from the cold, starvation, typhus, smallpox or all of them combined. I passed a mother with two children huddled up against her like animals, for the last warmth she could give; some passerby, taking pity, had tossed an oriental rug over them and then gone on his way. A demented woman sat on the roadside counting and recounting her fingers. The weather had turned more sharply cold, and adults and children walked along side or rode on rough carts, the ancient buggies, the rusted sleighs, with frostbitten feet and fingers.*

(Aten, 1961, p.202 & 210.)

**"We arrived at Rostov at 6pm on Sunday 6th Jan. 1920 & left at 8pm on the same date."**

Rostov was deserted, houses and shops were boarded up, but the hospital jammed with thousands of typhus sufferers. Though my granddad includes little detail of the mass retreat he does give us a thumbnail sketch of a scene that conveys the horror of it.

**"Just outside Rostov station we saw two men hanging from a tree who had been hanged by the Russian army for distributing Bolshevik propaganda. While one of them was being hanged his brains were blown out by a Russian officer. It was a terrible sight to see."**

The Red Terror was a program of executions carried out by the Red Army, officially in 1918 but extending for the whole period of the Civil War. These executions were aimed at all political enemies of the Bolsheviks. In effect it was a carte blanche for everyone and anyone to kill anyone they didn't like. The regime afterwards would blame the 100,000 plus executions on over-excited peasants. There was a corresponding White Terror so hangings and shootings must have been common sights. It led unsurprisingly to retaliatory acts of vengeance by victorious troops too, in some cases the cause and effect only being hours apart. Perhaps the 17 hanging men seen by B Flight at Rostov, according to Aten (p.227), were seen on January 6th rather than News Year's Eve? Both Major H.N.H Williamson in *Farewell to the Don* and John T. Smith in *Gone to Russia to Fight*, mentions the hanging of people, both men and women, in Rostov, in their books. Smith is quoting the unpublished papers of a Wing Commander Jenks who was on one of the last trains out of Rostov c. January 5$^{th}$ (Smith, Chapter 17). Williamson, in *Farewell to the Don* states that the hanging an attempt by the commander of Rostov to restore order (p.247). Granddad adds...

*"About two hours after we left Rostov the Cossack Brigade which was to defend the town turned Bolshevik and murdered all the loyal Russian soldiers & handed the town over to the Bolshies."*

This entry casts some more doubt on dates. Though B Flight were said to have left Rostov on the 9<sup>th</sup> could they have left in fact on the 6<sup>th</sup>? We may never know now.

Rostov was in Don Cossack territory which had recently been declared a Republic. Under General Mamontov they had been strong allies of the White Army. However General Mamontov had been removed by Denikin, a move which served to alienate the Cossack troops and obviously brought natural tensions between White officers and Cossacks violently to a head.

## Ekaterodinar

Twelve days on a train in freezing, disease-ridden conditions hardly bears thinking about. The steppe would have been littered with bodies of both people and animals as well as streams of live refugees struggling south by sleigh, cart and on weary feet. Major Williamson describes it…

*Dead horses, abandoned wagons, guns and equipment blocked the roads. Thousands of wounded died untended when hospitals were evacuated and they were hurried to the railway on improvised stretchers, only to succumb to cold or lack of care…the Army [White] were utterly exhausted. Skeleton regiments trudged southwards, their feet wrapped in cloth and sack, artillerymen dragging their rusted guns, the exhausted men falling from their horses to freeze to death before they woke.* (Williamson, p.256).

Some refugees would try to hitch a ride on the trains. One account tells of an overloaded train pulling out of a station its roof crowded with clinging evacuees. When morning came, they were gone, pushed or fallen from their perches after freezing to death.

*"We arrived at Ekaterinodar at 10pm on Monday 12th Jan. 1920 & left at 11pm on the same date."*

Ekaterinodar, now Krasnodar, was where the White Army headquarters had been at the very start of the Volunteer Army offensive. It was here Denikin, and his fellow generals had fled from the Bolshevik revolution, here the Volunteer Army had formed and here Denikin was appointed overall chief. It was here also that the British, in the form of Lieutenant-Colonel Blackwood and a small mission, made first official contact with General Denikin in November 1918 to discuss the British Intervention. Since then, all those plans had disintegrated. In his book *Churchill's Secret War...* Wright recounts how Holman addressed his men at Ekaterinodar. Though he is hazy on the dates, according to John Smith in *Gone to Russia to Fight*, Holman had been in a Z Flight plane that crashed landed at Ekaterinodar on January 11th, so Holman's address was most likely on that date. Holman was concerned about the White Russian refugees who were being abandoned by their Army, but he could not officially order the 900 men of the Military Mission - the only bulwark between the Bolsheviks and the refugees - to stay and escort the Whites. Instead, that day, he offered his men a chance to leave for Novorossiysk immediately. Three did. The rest stayed until the following day, January 12th, the date granddad's train came through. Then, the refugees, both civilian and soldiers, were loaded into already packed trains or carts and sleighs and sent south with a British Army escort. Granddad's train, arriving at 10pm, the last carrying members of the British Military Mission back to Novorossiysk before the Red Tide came in, must have been part of that escort. The Bolsheviks, suffering the same over extended lines the Whites had months previously, would not take Ekaterinodar until March 1920. Typically, General Holman, would be the last to leave that city on March 15th, the Whites long gone. But there were still the Caucasian mountains to cross before the Mission men were safely in Novorossiysk.

*"An order was issued at 1am on Tuesday 13th Jan. 1920 to the effect that all men were to stand by with loaded rifles while we were crossing the Caucasian Mountains in case were attacked by the Green Guards."*

door of our billet froz
...ath. At 10 am. on Mo...
Feb. 1920 we saw abou...
... of the Green Guards ...
... been captured by ...
...ck patrol. They we...
...ched into the town
...licly shot. On Wed. 2...
1920 one of our light
...ers the "H.M.S. Steadfa...
...shelled by a land
...ery of the Green Guar...
... the coast before s...
...tered Novorossisk. Th...
... two casualties on bo...
...ship was only sligh...

# Chapter Eight: Novorossiysk

NOVOROSSISK, EARLY 20TH CENTURY. PHOTOGRAPHER UNKNOWN

## The Green Guards

*"The hills which surround Novorossisk are infested by a band of brigands known as the Green Guards. When these Green Guards go short of stores they come down into the town & loot it. "*

Of the players in the war my granddad mentions, it is the Green Guards who appear most often. As he spent the majority of his time in Novorossiysk that is no surprise. While the enemy in the form of 'Bolshies' were on the other side of the line, the Green Guards were everywhere in southeast Russia. My granddad describes them here...

*"The Green Guards are mainly composed of deserters from the Bolshevik and Russian armies & they number about 17,000."*

It is quite good summing up from someone on the ground in a chaotic situation, or even afterwards, as in the early 1920s accurate information would have been impossible to come by. A report from the Donburo, a Soviet administration for the 'free' parts of the Don district from September 1919, states that the Green Army began with a group of Red Army deserters who found themselves a hideout in the mountains in 1918 though other reports say the Greens began with a loose coalition of peasants whose food and livestock were often taken by soldiers of both armies. However, many Red Army soldiers had been forced to join up, leaving their homes and farms to fight for something they didn't really have anything to do with. When they deserted, peasants began to gather around these men, some of whom had good leadership qualities. Deserters from both sides continued to swell their ranks and included some Communist units. The Red Army recorded between 20,000 and 50,000 desertions per month in 1919 and the White Army were sometimes reduced to trying to recruit Bolshevik prisoners. The Green Guards had a big impact on the course of the War. The Greens had assisted the White advance unintentionally by harassing the Bolsheviks and some historians believe that they impacted the Soviet policy, but the Green Guards harassed the White Army too causing chaos in Denikin's rear, which, combined with Makhno's Black Army incursions, forced Denikin to withdraw south. When the Red Army realised the size of the Green Army, they wanted to harness it but could not. The Greens would nearly capture Novorossiysk at least twice in the first months of 1920. They were able to field at least 70,000 men at their peak. They must have been very hardy to spend the winter in the mountains with temperatures dropping to well below zero. While they used weapons that they had brought or captured from various armies, they were also funded by the Georgian government who, like so many, were intent on keeping their independence rather than be united under a Soviet or White Russia.

A further report from the Donburo divided the Green Guards into three regional groups. One that operated on the coast 200km south of Novorossiysk, and two groups in and around Novorossiysk. These groups were further split up into bands of between 2,000 and 4,000 men under varying qualities of leaders. Kopisto says that the Green Guards around Novorossiysk at this point numbered between 5000 and 6000 and Novorossiysk was now the key city, for both White and Red.

*"During the time we were in Novorossisk we were very often turned out of bed in the early hours of the morning to guard our stores owing to the Green Guards coming down from the hills to loot the town."*

The night temperature at one point during these months was at minus 45 degrees.

*"At 5am on Sat 7th Feb. 1920 one of our warships called the 'Benbow' left the harbour and sailed down the coast & bombarded the haunts of the Green Guards which were about three miles from our billet."*

In this instance 150 Russian soldiers and a British officer on a reconnaissance mission had been fired upon and taken refuge in a village seven miles down the coast from Novorossiysk. The British officer had been wounded and several others too. The *Benbow* pulverized a village in retaliation which was meant to finally stop the Greens sniping at the soldiers in Novorossiysk but as, we shall see, the Greens soon got their mojo back.

## The Benbow

The *Benbow,* the third of four Iron Class Duke, was laid down in 1912 and launched just after the start of the Great War. There were four in this class. At 25,000 tons they measured 190 x 28 x9 metres and would carry roughly 1000 crew. Present at The Battle of Jutland in 1916 but seeing little action, the *Benbow* was assigned to the Mediterranean Fleet after the war. The *Benbow*, like the *Steadfast* carried a lot of the players back and forth in the Black Sea as well as patrolling the shores. After being reassigned to the Atlantic Fleet in the mid 20s she was sold for scrap in 1931 It is notable that often the smaller, probably cheaper, cargo and passenger vessels had longer lives than the purpose built war-machines.

FIG. 18. THE BENBOW UNDERWAY, JANUARY 1917. PHOTOGRAPHER: UNKNOWN/PUBLIC DOMAIN, SOURCE: IWM

*"At 10am on Mon. 16th Feb. 1920 we saw about 150 of the Green Guards who had been captured by Cossack patrol. They were marched into the town and publicly shot."*

The Cossacks had been known to drag prisoners behind their horses with predictably horrific results, so shooting these Green Guards was quite merciful in context. Maybe the British, who had long been objecting to Denikin's wholesale execution of Red Army prisoners, had been bringing pressure to bear because of Red Army torture rumours. These rumours were so rife that many officers, including British ones, carried poison capsules or grenades to kill themselves in the event of capture.

A report from the Donburo stated that there was a growing and 'enormous' number of Red Army prisoners of war at Novorossiysk held in appalling conditions, so it is possible there just was no room - and no time - to do anything more elaborate than shoot those Green Guards. This Cossack patrol could have been Don Cossacks who had retreated from the Don area with the Whites. The Kuban Cossacks of the area were at loggerheads with Denikin, probably because of the tension between Denikin and their commander, General Wrangel.

*"On Wed. 25th Feb. 1920 one of our light cruisers the "H.M.S. Steadfast" was shelled by a land battery of the Green Guards along the coast before she entered Novorossisk. There were two casualties on board and the ship was only slightly damaged."*

The *Benbows*' village pulverisation had done little to soften the cough of the Greens and attacks continued.

*"On Wed. 10th Mar. 1920 we were turned out of bed at 2am because the Green Guards attacked a party of our men who were sleeping close to the aerodrome which was about five miles away from our billet & took their rifles & machine gun & ammunition. A small boat was sent out from one of our warships called "The Emperor of India" which was lying in the harbour & took our men on board where they stopped until morning. A party of marines were also landed but the Green Guards were gone."*

This looks to be a major incident but I could find no other account of it. *The Emperor of India*, like the *Benbow,* was an Iron Duke class Dreadnought. The size of these ships might give some idea of the threat the Green Guards posed. Once the Bolsheviks won, and famine intensified, the Green Guards would dissolve, the peasants making their way home. They would have all but disappeared within a couple of years. But right now, in January 1920, though it may have been some distance from the front proper, Novorossiysk was not a particularly safe place to be. Granddad arrived there nearly two weeks after leaving Taganrog 500km away.

*"We arrived at Novorossisk at 12 noon on Tuesday 13th Jan. 1920 after being twelve days in the train during which time we only travelled about 500 miles. A fast passenger train can do the journey in three days. We left the train and arrived at base depot at 3pm on Thursday 15th Jan. 1920."*

While he mentions little of that journey, he does include a teaser...

*"During the retreat I shared my rations with a Russian Princess who was a refugee".*

No story is complete without a Princess.

### A Princess & a Marriage

Was there a Princess on the train among the refugees? It's more than possible. The Romanovs along with other families of the aristocracy had become targets of the Bolsheviks when they were classified as 'former people' after the November Revolution. The Romanovs were the Royal family and its head, the Tsar Nicolas, and his immediate family were murdered by the Bolsheviks at Ekaterinburg in July 1918. The aristocracy were forced to live on starvation rations which they would only receive if they had proof they were working. Russian princesses were forced to clean public toilets or shovel snow while Tsarist generals were made move rocks from one place to another for no particular reason. The last of the Romanov family would flee from the Crimea in 1920. It would be no surprise to find a princess or a noble woman on a refugee train sharing a soldier's rations, which may, after two years of starvation, have seemed like a feast to her. Indeed, B Flight's train, which was travelling the same retreat route as granddad, had a countess on board.

The only aristocrat who may have evacuated through Novorossiysk in this time is the Grand Duchess Olga Alexandrovna, youngest sister of the Tsar, thirty-eight at the time, who was fleeing with her second husband and two sons. They had been briefly living between Rostov and Ekaterinodar before they left Novorossiysk in February 1920 which is the right time frame.

However, to an Irish soldier any noble woman must have seemed like a princess and any woman would likely have pretended to be a princess too as women were in a desperate situation. There would be half a million refugees in Novorossiysk by March 1920. The British would manage to get only 50,000 out by March 22nd, when the last of the British left. So, if this lady was not Grand Duchess Olga Alexandrovna, it is possible she was a noble woman angling for a proposal. Our princess, crammed into a packed train creeping across a steppe littered with bodies in the depths of a Russian winter with probably only the clothes on her back and desperate for survival may have set her cap at one of granddad's comrades as later in the diary he mentions a wedding in Novorossiysk.

*"One of our officers was married to a Russian girl in Novorossisk & I was one of the guard of honour. We formed an archway with our rifles and bayonets for him and his bride to pass under."*

When I first read the diary some years ago it never crossed my mind this union was anything other than romantic but for a woman caught up in this great exodus the best way out was to marry a soldier. Major Williamson says in his account, *Farewell to the Don…*

*'Young girls were trying desperately to get themselves married to English men - not for love but to get out of the country as British subjects - and

*several actually did, making arrangements to part as soon as they were in safety.'* (Williamson, p.277)

There are no records of any marriages of British servicemen to Russian women, let alone the one my granddad attended but they must have been rushed affairs, celebrated by Russian orthodox priests or army or navy personnel, and may not have been recorded. It is telling that the soldier my granddad mentions is an officer. As we have seen, General Holman had said he would do all he could to make sure they and their families escaped Novorossiysk and had promised White Russian friends who get all their families safely onto British ships. This may have inspired his subordinates to follow his lead. Maybe officers were even asked to help. Having said that, it is also the case that Russian families desperate to save female family members were offering sums of money to any soldier who would marry them.

*'Distraught fathers offered money to British soldiers to marry their daughters, and young girls-some of high birth-prostituted themselves to earn enough money to pay the passage for themselves and their families to ruthless and money-grabbing barge captains...Invariably, even as they earned the money, the prices went up as others also clamoured for places, and some of the girls committed suicide.'* (Williamson, p.277)

To quote Williamson, this *'sick, desperate, terrified city'* would be granddad's home for the next two months.

## Duck!

*"Every evening in Novorossisk we used to go shooting wild ducks with our rifles on the coast of the Black Sea."*

Novorossiysk, early 1920. The area is cut off by an advancing Bolshevik Army. Roving bands of Green Guards numbering up to 6000 combined, armed to teeth, annoyed at everyone, and only quelled temporarily by being pulverized by a destroyer, are everywhere. Defences are down to some barricades the British have made and a White Army whose only intention is get themselves and their loot out. During this there is time for a spot of shooting.

While starvation was an issue for refugees it wasn't for the soldiers but though there would have been a surplus of rations, a lot of army food would have been tinned. Hard biscuits and tea were a staple, but that diet would get monotonous fairly fast. Fresh duck meat would have been very welcome in the winter of 1920. Hunting would have been a diversion too. The climate at Novorossiysk is classed as temperate but it was prone to some heavy winter weather.

> *"At one time on Novorossisk it was so cold that we could not leave the billet for four days & the thermometer showed us it was 45 degrees below zero."*

Though he does not date this it was probably around the beginning of February 1920. For comparison, an account of Shackleton's Endurance expedition mentions a regular temperature of minus 20 when the Endurance was stuck fast in the ice in Antarctica. Cold weather forces inland birds to come to the shore and during January on the Black Sea, migrant ducks would be passing on the way to Africa. Tsemes Bay at Novorossiysk did not freeze - though sometimes the entrance to the harbour did - making it a prime winter duck hunting spot. There is said to be over forty species of duck in Russia. While it is usual to put out decoy ducks, they wouldn't have had any. Further Googling turned up the nugget that it is 'traditional' on the Black Sea to shoot at flying ducks from speed boats, casting both peasants and the history of speed boats in a new light.

Growing up in East Wall in Dublin may not have provided granddad many opportunities to shoot though it's possible he went up the Dublin Mountains or out along the shore to shoot, and fish. Later, when he was a Garda in coastal County Wexford during World War II and meat was scarce, he, and his sons, would shoot rabbits for the table with a .22 rifle. Perhaps when he rested the stock of his rifle against his shoulder, sighting down the barrel at a bobbing scut weaving across a field, lemon and viridian in late afternoon on the Irish coast, he thought of the shores of the Black Sea on a dwindling day decades before. In an encircled city, to bundle up and step out alongside similarly wrapped fellows - barely recognisable from an inch or so of bright pink skin or an icy brow just visible - to prowl the foreign shore, plumes of breath in the crisp air, snow crunching underfoot, sky fading blue to yellow to pink, must have felt like stepping out of time. The sea, sluggish as blood, barely lapping the shore, the rasp of snow underfoot the only sounds in the stillness. The air so cold it would sear the skin, every inhalation, every exhalation burning as the fierce cold whittled the senses to a point, sending thoughts of the overcrowded port fluttering away into the silence. Then, the click-clack of a bolt, the tinny snap of a shot cracks the sky, breaking his train of thought and the bloodied rabbit is swept briskly up by a callous hand to swing, head down, keeping time with its executioner's stride. But he wasn't given much to fancies and if he ever thought of Russia at all, he never let anyone know.

**Frozen**

*"At 8am on Thursday 12th Feb. 1920 we found two men and one woman lying outside the door of our billet frozen to death."*

While the Green Guards hiding on the surrounding mountain were obviously quite hardy, for the refugees crowding into Novorossiysk the weather could be fatal. These undoubtedly weren't the first frozen bodies granddad had seen. Everyone would have been hardened to sights of war at this stage. Granddad had already seen men hung up on trees whose brains were shot out and he would have seen frozen bodies on the steppe from the twelve-day train ride at the tail end of the retreat from Taganrog. But these were probably the first that he, or at least his unit could have theoretically saved had they known these people were outside their door.

Marion Aten in *Last Train Over Rostov Bridge* describes retreating south from Debal'tseve to Taganrog in December 1919.

*'The refugee death rate climbed to fantastic heights. Every station had rows of frozen, unburied bodies and every morning at seven we would awaken to women's lamentations over a son, a husband a brother found dead.'*

(Aten, p.193)

There would be many, many more to be found in the streets of Novorossiysk. John T. Smith in *Gone to Russia to Fight* says thousands of bodies were found on the streets of Novorossiysk each morning. Major Williamson in *Farewell to the Don* describes Novorossiysk at this time...

*It was freezingly cold. Bodies lay in all sorts of corners, while hospitals were besieged by sick, frozen and hungry people for whom nothing could be done, so that those stricken with typhus remained where they fell. One Russian colonel lay for a fortnight in a cupboard where he had crept when he had taken ill.* (Williamson, p.276)

In the early part of the twentieth century, disposal of bodies was a massive problem in Russia even in urban areas and especially in winter. In Moscow and Petrograd piles of bodies lay decomposing or eaten by vermin in cemetery sheds. Even when the ground softened there was little room left. Bodies were eventually carted hours out of the cities, and sometimes buried in mass graves, distance and lack of identification denying relatives a grave to visit. In the winter of 1920, the ground would have been too hard to dig any graves. Out on the steppe many bodies were thrown or fell from moving trains. In Novorossiysk there seems to have been no concerted action to clear bodies. Later, when Wrangel took over leadership of the White Army in the Crimea he managed to impose some law and order which presumably included sanitation services too but that was two months off and Denikin was still in charge at Novorossiysk and chaos reigned.

Some may have considered those who froze as being lucky. After the departure of the British and the last of the Whites under Wrangel in the Crimea in late 1920, an estimated seven million peasants would starve in the ensuing famine. Cannibalism became common and body parts were openly sold in marketplaces. Some people retained the bodies of their relatives for food while others exhumed bodies to eat them. Aside from the immediate health problems, both physical and mental, that would have been born from of all of the above scenarios, the difficulty in respecting the dead along with the Bolshevik rebuttal of all that was religious would have long-term negative impact on the people of Russia. In this country with great attachment to rituals, the minimization of them would lead to the minimization of feelings, the cheapening of human life and a huge psychological burden on an already devastated nation.

peror of India whi
lying in the harbo
our men on boar
they stopped until
-g. A party of marin
also landed but
reen Guards had
On Sun. 21ˢᵗ Mar. 192
ceived ~~only~~ orders to evacu
sisk. By Tuesday 23
20 we had packed
early all our stores
broken up all ou
s, both air & motor,
ll preparations ma

# Chapter Nine: Evacuation

## The British Prepare to Leave

*"On Sun. 21st Mar. 1920 we received orders to evacuate Novorossisk. By Tuesday 23rd Mar. 1920 we had packed up nearly all our stores & had broken up all our engines, both air and motor & had all our preparations made for the evacuation."*

The events in Taganrog and other cities had convinced the British that the White troops could not be trusted to obey orders, so the British took over the command of this last evacuation. In the absence of any coherent plan from the White Army officers, members of the British Mission were armed and organized to defend their base and the harbour of Novorossiysk. Trenches had been dug, machine gun posts and barbed wire were installed at key points. In the two weeks leading up to the evacuation the 2nd Battalion of Royal Scots Fusiliers under Lieutenant Colonel R. K. Walsh who had also fought at the Somme (Walsh is a good Waterford name however I could find no other information on R.K.), were shipped in from Constantinople where they were based. General Holman had pledged to evacuate the families of the White soldiers. A decision my granddad noted in his account...

*"A few days before the evacuation one of our generals named General Holman promised the Russian General Denikin that the British Troops would see that all the women and children*

*were got away safely which we did alright & were nearly being captured ourselves over getting them away first."*

General Holman, though still head of the British Military Mission, had been placed by Churchill under the direct orders of General Milne, the commander of the British forces on the Black Sea, in January 1920. Churchill did this because of Holman's 'strong feelings for the Whites'. General Milne put General Sir Thomas Bridges in charge of the nitty gritty of the evacuation. Bridges, less embedded in the situation, would describe Holman as being more concerned with supporting Denikin's cause than with the safety of his own men. Bridges had wanted to withdraw the Mission straight to Constantinople in early 1920 in view of Denikin's lack of involvement in defending Novorossiysk but Holman insisted on supporting Denikin and the evacuation of the Russians. By the end of February, General Holman had instructed the unloading of supplies to be stopped at Novorossiysk and transferred to the Crimea where General Wrangel would direct the last of the White resistance. The 'Bolshies' had taken Ekaterinodar on March 18th and Holman would be last to leave that city.

The evacuation would be a difficult chore for the British Mission. They managed to register and evacuate 50,000 refugees by March 22nd but on the weeks leading up to the final departure date of March 26th, the town was heaving with a mind-boggling estimated 500,000 unregistered refugees some of whom had travelled a thousand miles to escape and who were now clogging the city and docks in their desperation to get away. Many of them would fail to do so. Not only did the British have to organise an impossible evacuation but the supplies they had brought, much of which had not reached the frontlines, were scattered about the docks and had to be destroyed or pushed into the harbour. Among these refugees there were the soldiers; the British, the Whites but also the Cossacks with their horses, the Don and the Kuban. Major Williamson vividly describes the mood of the soldiers…

*'Troops were throwing away their shoulder straps and officers tearing off their epaulettes because the Reds… liked to indulge in the pleasant practice of nailing them to their wearer's shoulders when captured… while others shot themselves in despair.'* (Williamson, p.277)

They were right to be afraid. My granddad notes in his account that after the last of the Mission sailed…

**"There were four hundred Russian officers left behind & these were all cut-up by the Bolshies."**

Suicide would not be uncommon during these weeks. White Army soldiers would kill their families and themselves on the shores of the Black Sea as the last transports disappeared over the horizon.

The following is from an unverified but descriptive account found online and translated from Russian.

*Many of the remaining Novorossiysk officers of the Armed Forces of Southern Russia have committed suicide, not wanting to be captured, and many of those ...captured - were executed...I remember [a] Captain [of] Drozdowski Regiment, standing not far from me, with his wife and two children, three and five years. Crossed himself and kissed them, he shoots each of them in the ear, baptizing his wife in tears saying goodbye to her; and, behold, shot, she falls, and the last bullet in itself...*

FIG. 19. LIEUTENANT COLONEL BINGHAM.

British soldiers were far from unaffected by the terrible situation. Many already carried the means to do away with themselves, in the form of cyanide pills, for fear of capture by the Bolsheviks. A Lieutenant Colonel Bingham OBE of the 69th Punjabis, had served during the Boxer rebellion in China, as General Holman had, and survived Gallipoli was in charge of transport in Novorossiysk. He suicided with his service revolver on March 18th. Bingham was anguished by orders at having to turn away refugees who were not related to any military personnel, rightly fearing many would be murdered by the Bolsheviks. Despite his orders, before his death he would manage to save several civilian families. He was 42. He is buried at Novorossiysk and remembered on the Haidar Pasha monument at Constantinople.*

* Finnish Blogger Mathias Luther who is himself writing about the same era, informs me that the house where Bingham shot himself was also the one where his grandfather was staying along with other British Officers. You can find his blog address at the end of the book.

The British tried their best to keep order. Novorossiysk was nominally under the command of a Russian military governor and the commander of the fort, but they were at loggerheads and less than useless. The city could have been protected, possibly indefinitely as it was surrounded by the mountains and sea and there was only one road and one railway into the town through a narrow ravine. But there were no White troops available to post anywhere. Of any remaining units, Denikin was reluctant to sacrifice them as he was planning to regroup in the Crimea. The British Mission at this point numbered around 1458 - the most men it would have in South Russia - with 356 of those being officers - and they had their hands full keeping order, trying to save the families of Russian soldiers and breaking down the mountain of supplies. The Royal Scots Fusiliers guarding the docks would be swarmed by the desperate horde of refugees whom they threw back at bayonet point at least once.

In an attempt to calm the situation and boost morale General Bridges decided to have a parade of all available soldiers and marines including a band and some pipers. In a city where thousands of people were found dead on the streets each morning, where people were selling everything they had to try to get out, a city under attack by the Greens and the Reds and echoing with rifle fire and naval shot hurled from the British destroyers in the harbour, the concussion of guns, according to Williamson, *'beating against the ears and rattling windows in the houses,'* the parade must have been surreal. It would be the last celebratory show many would see for a long time or ever again for that matter.

During the evacuation, the British battleship *Emperor of India* and the French cruiser *Waldeck Rousseau* would provide covering fire, shelling Budenny's Bolshevik cavalry who were outside the port. By the 26th of March 1920 the Green Guards were getting bolder while the local Bolsheviks, who were already murdering and raping in the town, had also cut up several parties of Kalmyk Cossacks trying to get through to the port. Williamson writes that at least one half of the troops fighting the rear-guard action against the vast Red Army were Don Cossacks, having stuck it out far longer than the 'ornamental' Kuban Cossacks, as he refers to them. During the night of the 26th of March 1920, General Holman would stand on the mole of the harbour supervising the embarkation of his beloved Don Cossacks. General Denikin in wanting to preserve the remnants of the Volunteer army for the last stand in the Crimea, had rushed his soldiers to the ships leaving the Don Cossacks behind.

*'The Cossack troops had arrived at Novorossiysk with their horses; when they were told that there was no room for the horses on the ships, they shot them rather than allow them to fall into the hands of the Reds. The docks became littered with thousands of dead horses.*

(Smith, 2010, Chapter 19)

Some of them would swim their horses out to the ships and climb on board leaving their mounts to drown. The harbour was full of their bloated bodies. As with the panic of the refugees, my granddad makes no mention of horse's bodies on or in the harbour or of swimming Cossacks, but he does refer to the live horses left onshore in a paragraph that leaves a dramatic after-image…

**"The Russian army left Novorossisk for Crimea ten hours before we did. The British troops were last to evacuate & our party sailed on the last troop ship. The Russian Army before sailing for Crimea let all their horses go loose in the town. "**

For the Cossack, absorbed into the Soviet experiment, the devastating choice between their horses and their own lives at Novorossiysk reflected a greater loss: centuries of independence, a wide-open steppe, freedom, and home. The horses, long-limbed, elegant black cut-outs against the backdrop of a roiling red inferno, manes and tails like inverted flames and fringed with fire as they galloped here and there, desperate to find a way to freedom, destined to fail. It is a powerful image that captures the violence of the red tide and the voraciousness with which it consumed the freedom of all those that fled before it.

## Civilians

Novorossiysk was flooded with civilians from all points north, many of whom had no connection to the Volunteer Army. Some may have managed to pay their way on board one of the ships that had left in the last few weeks, with money or with favours or the favours of their daughters. They would have gone to the Crimea where Wrangel would hold out until November before evacuating 146,000 people - both army and civilian - to Turkey and then to Belgrade. Some would have gone straight to Constantinople and then dispersed west, part of the largest refugee diaspora in modern history up to that time. Far more would not have been so lucky.

*'It was a sick, desperate, terrified city with mobs of people surging to every point where they thought there might be hope of safety or evacuation. Amid horses, camels, wagons and supplies, they raised their hands to the ship masters knowing their only alternative to evacuation was death when the Bolshevik cavalry arrived. They even tried to fight their way aboard ships, and when they failed simply succumbed to cold and despair in a numb*

*blank-eyed silence as they huddled over their belongings, all hope gone, all desire to live long vanished.'*

(Williamson, p.277)

By mid-March 1920 most civilian ships had left and in the last week there would be little hope of escape by sea. Some must have survived though. The local prostitutes, many of whom had dressed in British nurse's uniforms procured from the mountains of supplies that had so recently poured into Novorossisk, would probably have already left since their business was undercut by the hordes of incoming refugees. Some would have evaded death by the necessity to keep the city operational and by being clever enough to support whoever happened to be in power. Then there were those who were hardy enough to melt into the surrounding hills and join the Green Guards for the time being.

Major Williamson says…

*'The strong survived as they always did, because they were ruthless and didn't mind what they did to survive, but the weak died in thousands upon thousands.'* (Williamson, p.281)

Bridges, in charge of destroying British supplies on the Novorossiysk dock could not in the end bring himself to destroy the food, clothing and boats there in the presence of the refugees suffering, left them as a present to the Bolsheviks. It is hard to say how many died. A couple of sources say it was in the thousands and though it pales relative to the 3 million who would die of typhus in Russia that year and the further 6 million who would die in the ensuing year of famine. But, to a person on that quayside, crushed by a mindless mob, a person carried helpless to the edge and then over it to sink into the bitterly cold sea of Tsemes Bay, relativity would have meant very little. Damien Wright in his book *Churchill's Secret War* ...includes this description from Russian Nobel Prize Konstantin Paustovsky winning writer in Volume 3 of his *Story of a Life*. Wright says that Paustovsky was on the Novorossiysk docks but in fact it was Odessa in February of 1920 he was describing. However, the description may reflect something of Novorossiysk which was a month nearer total Bolshevik takeover.

'For a very long time afterward, I was haunted and burdened by the feeling that at some time, in some picture by a pitiless artist, I had already witnessed this epic flight; gaping mouths, torn open by cries for help, eyes bulging from their sockets, faces livid and deeply etched by fear of death, of people who could see nothing but the one, blinding, terrible sight: rickety ships gangplanks with hand rails snapping under the weight of human bodies, soldier's rifles butts crashing down overhead, mothers stretching up their arms to lift their children above the demented human herd, the children desperately crying, and the trampled body of a woman still squirming and screaming on the quay.'

'People were senselessly destroying each other, preventing even those who reached the gangway from saving themselves. The moment anyone gained hold on the plank or the rail, hands grabbed and clutched at him, clusters of bodies hung on him. He inched his way forward, pulling them along, but lost his hold, fell together with his terrible human load into the sea and drowned, powerless to shake it off...

...suitcases, bundles and baskets slithered downhill under foot, like monstrous living creatures. Clothes spilled out and wound themselves around shoes and ankles. Women's petticoats and lace, children's frocks and ribbons trailed after the fugitives, and the sight of these homely things made their flight even more tragic...'

(Paustovsky in Wright, p.424)

Of this hellish scene my granddad only writes...

*"...we were nearly being captured ourselves over getting them away first."*

### A Lovely Sight..

*"On Sun. 21st Mar. 1920 we received orders to evacuate Novorossisk. By Tuesday 23rd Mar. 1920 we had packed up nearly all our stores & had broken up all our engines, both air and motor & had all our preparations made for the evacuation. After blowing up our ammunition dump & setting fire to all our stores we hadn't time to take with us, we went on board the "H.M.S. Hanover" at 2:30pm on Friday 26th Mar. 1920 & sailed at 11:30pm on the same date."*

The docks were scattered with every conceivable type of military equipment at this point and the Army Service Corps were working in shifts to push container after container of supplies into the Black Sea. Two Sopwith Camels had been brought to Novorossiysk on board the *Baron Beck* and they were assembled ready to fly in an emergency. The long, straight breakwater at the entrance to the harbour was the intended runway but the Camels were dismantled on 26 March and shipped out. A number of Sopwirth Camels, RE8s and DH9s were deliberately crushed under the tracks of a tank which was then driven off the end of the wharf. Being attached to the RAF granddad would probably have been party to the destruction of the planes on the docks, some, it was claimed in *Last Train Over Rostov Bridge*, were still in their crates. The perishables were left to the refugees and the Bolsheviks.

FIG.20. NOVOROSSISK, MARCH 1920. PHOTOGRAPHER UNKNOWN. SOURCE: WIKIPEDIA.

B Flight left the same night as my granddad who was on the last ship out. B Flight were part of 4000 men on the *Baron Beck*, which had berths for only 1500, while granddad was with the British Mission on board the *HMT Hannover*.

*"Our ship left harbour under shell fire from the Bolshie guns. The Bolshies started shelling ships in the harbour and sunk one foreign ship. One of our warships named the "Emperor of India" & some of our destroyers which were in the harbour*

shelled the hills all round Novorossisk where the Bolshies were & then they blew up the town. "

On that last day *The Emperor of India* was joined by the French cruiser the *Waldeck Rousseau*, in lobbing huge shells at the Red Army as they came into the town. In the chaos snipers shot at each other and at civilians from the roof tops while a massive black cloud of smoke from the burning stores blocked out the sun. My granddad suggests it was the burning oil wells that created the smoke.

*"When our ship was lying outside the harbour all the oil-wells which surrounded the town were on fire & there was hardly a house standing"*

Then comes one of the strangest lines in the account. Here, at what sounds like the end of all things, with the sun extinguished first by smoke and then by flaming night, the choking air punctuated with the cries of those desperate to be rescued and of the dying, the waters of the harbour dotted with the bodies of people and horses, granddad stands on the crowded deck looking back at the devastated city and writes...

*"It was a lovely sight to see."*

Granddad was, like many men of his time, quite detached from his feelings, maybe even more so than most. Even though he spent the rest of his life as a Garda, embedded in the small communities he served, he remained very self-contained, distant even. This little notebook is the only clue to any feelings he might have had at this time. On board the SS *Hannover*, after months of tension, waiting to be attacked, being attacked, seeing misery and death everywhere, to see the whole thing go up in flames as one sailed safely out of reach must have caused a feeling of release in those watching though they would have been aware too of the fate of many of those souls they were leaving behind. The worst had happened, and they had survived. He was far from the first to be awed or inspired by war. Some of the School of London painters were influenced by the ruins left by The Blitz, and, in Joseph Heller's Catch 22, as Milo and Yossarian watch their base in flames, Milo, echoing granddad, exclaims…

*'Ain't it Beautiful!'*

Konstantin Paustovsky's account of the last evacuation at Odessa the previous month ends...

*'Suddenly the docks emptied. People hurled themselves back into the alleys, into the chinks of the port. Riding slowly down the slope littered with broken baggage, torn clothes and here and there a body trampled to death, came a Soviet mounted patrol. The men rode with their heads bowed, as though lost in thought. They pulled up beside the bodies, dismounted and bent over them, trying to see if any were alive - but none were. The horsemen rode to the end of the breakwater, halted and for a long time watched the ships.'*

(Paustovsky in Wright, p.424)

ould see that all
omen & children were
way safely which we
right & were nearly
ptured ourselves over
etting them away firs
fter sailing from Novor
the "H.M.T. Hanover
rived at Theodosia w
in Crimea at 10 am
aturday 27th Mar. 19
t 11 am. on Sun. 28th
20. we were taken fo
route march round
own of Theodosia. At
the same date Gen

# Chapter Ten: The Journey Home

## Theodosia

*"After sailing from Novorossisk on the "H.M.S. Hanover" we arrived at Theodosia which is in Crimea at 10am on Saturday 27th Mar. 1920. At 11am on Sun. 28th Mar. 1920 we were taken for a route march round the town of Theodosia. At 2pm on the same date General Holman called us altogether on the quayside and thanked us for the good work we done while serving in Russia."*

Theodosia was on the south-east coast of the Crimea and was described by one soldier stationed there as 'not unlike Lyme Regis'. The British Mission in the Crimea was smaller and would be headed by Brigadier General Percy when General Holman returned to Britain.

*"We sailed from Theodosia on the same troopship at 5:30am on Monday 27th March 1920 and disembarked at Constantinople at 12 noon on Sat. 3rd April 1920. We arrived at Maslak Rest Camp at 4:30pm on the same date. During our stay in this camp a case of typhus broke out and we were all kept in quarantine isolation for three weeks."*

## The H.M.S Hannover

The most likely candidate for granddad's *'Hanover'* is the *Hannover*, a passenger/cargo ship begun a week before granddad was born in 1899 and finished in November that year. It was built on Tyneside by Wigham Richardson & Co for Norddeutscher Lloyd, Bremen. In 1919 the *Hannover* was given to Britain as part of war reparations but returned to its previous owners in 1922 and broken up in 1933. For a ship that is mentioned in many accounts of the evacuation of Novorossisk, its role there is not noted in any of its histories.

FIG. 21. HMS HANNOVER'S, PHOTO: PHOTOSHIP.

**The Fez**

He was on the way home, but his adventures were not over. Maslak camp was in what is now the Maslak business district of Istanbul which is on the European side of the city and close to the Bosphorus.

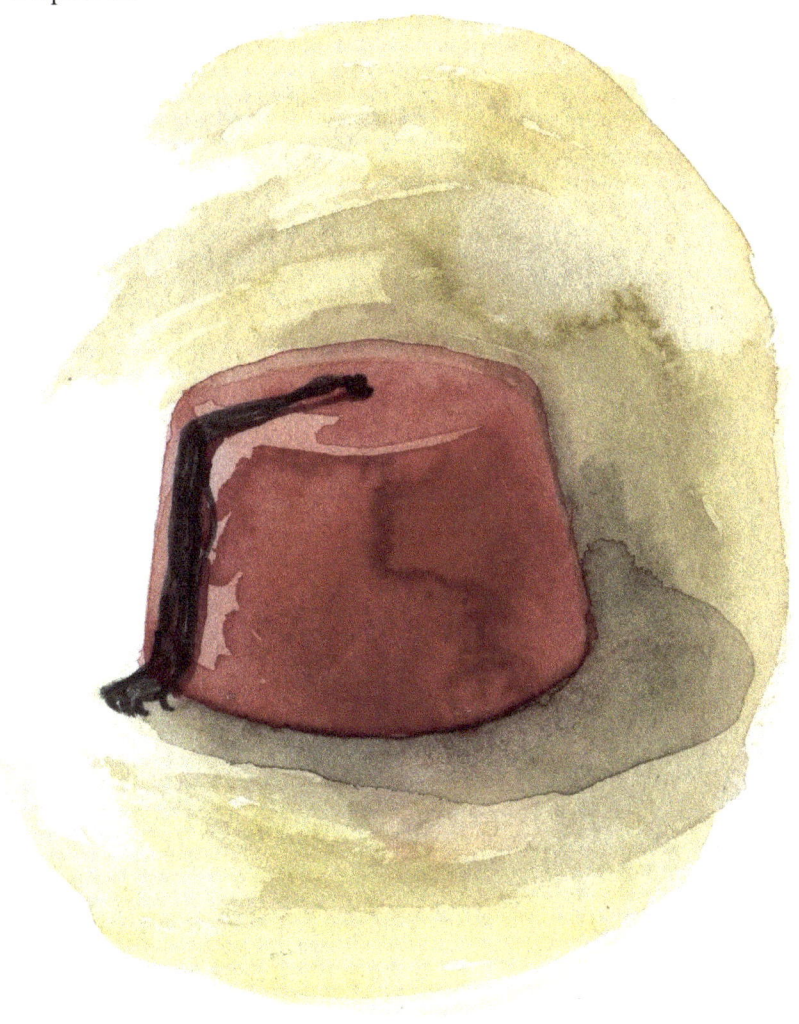

The last time granddad had passed through Constantinople areas of the city had been closed off because of the plague. Now he was quarantined. But there was still time for a tour before they left.

*"On the 29th April 1920 we had a tour round several villages on the shores of the Bosphorus in a small boat."*

No doubt some refreshments were imbibed which may explain some of what happened next…

*"When we were coming back to camp that night we stopped a Turkish taxicab driver & asked him to drive us back to camp & he refused so I pulled out my revolver & and made him drive us back to camp with the barrel of the revolver pointing at his head. When we arrived at the camp I took his fez (which is a Turkish cap) for a souvenir."*

A band of young men having just been released from quarantine after months in a perilous and tense situation in a foreign country would have no qualms about pulling out their guns and the unfortunate taxi driver may have been familiar with this sort of situation too. Revolvers are a recurring theme in my granddad's life and probably in the lives of most young men in this turbulent century. It doesn't really excuse my granddad's behaviour though.

Fezzes were originally made in Fez in Morocco, the red colour coming from berries that grew only there. By the early 20th century Austria had become the main fez manufacturer. And the fez, once a symbol of modernity was a sign of old traditions and backwardness. However, Europeans and Christians in 1920 in Constantinople would wear fezzes as a symbol of respect and obedience for the Muslim rulers. If this is the case my granddad's robbing of the fez could conceivably have put an unfortunate taxi driver in even more danger. The fez would be banned by Ataturk in 1925 five years after my granddad liberated 'his' fez from its original owner.

Granddad supposedly brought the fez back from Constantinople. His oldest son Billy swore blind that he remembered it. Billy, who died in April 2018 at the age of ninety, was a raconteur who, in the interests of entertainment, embellished some of his stories so maybe he made up remembering the fez. If it was brought back, it is most likely is sitting gathering dust in some dark bar in one of the counties granddad was posted after he joined An Garda Síochána (the Irish Police force) in 1923. A fez would have been a grand talking point down the pub and maybe even worth a few large bottles of Guinness.

## Chanak & Kantara

*"After a stay of five weeks in Constantinople we sailed for Port Said, Egypt at 3pm on Sunday 9th May 1920 on the "H.M.S. Hanover" the same troopship that brought us from Russia to Constantinople. We arrived at Port Said at 8am on Friday 14th May 1920 & landed at 11am on Sat 15th May 1920. When we were on our way to Port Said from Constantinople, we dropped anchor at a place called Chanak at the mouth of the Dardanelles to let some troops go ashore who were stationed there. While we were at anchor one of our anchor chains snapped & we had to stop there two hours extra while a diver looked for the anchor but he couldn't find it so we had to sail without it."*

Chanak (now called Canakkale), a small seaport on the Dardanelles strait Chanak would be in the news two years later for what would be called the Chanak Crisis. Under the Treaty of Sevres, which was imposed on Turkey following its defeat in the First World War, military forces from Britain, France and Greece occupied large portions of western Turkey. In the fall of 1922, nationalist Turkish forces, which opposed the presence of foreign troops, had succeeded in pushing the Greek army out of the country. The Turks then threatened British forces pinned down at Chanak. This situation led to the fall of prime minister, Lloyd George, who had been against British interference in Russia.

*"After landing at Port Said we entrained at 1pm on the same date for the demobilization camp at Kantara & arrived there at 3:30pm. The camp at Kantara was right in the middle of the burning sandy desert near the Suez Canal. After spending a period of three weeks at Kantara we left at 6am on Thursday 10th June 1920 & arrived at Port Said at 8am on the same date."*

And that is all we hear about Kantara or El Qantara. W.J. Cording whom we heard from earlier in the book, passed this way in late 1918. He was there for three months and has nothing much to say about it either. He does not even mention his beloved food except for saying that Kantara was in the 'dessert' [sic]. According to A.E. Williams, a private in the Army Cyclist Corps In 1916, Kantara resembled...

'...a western cow-town. Tents, marquees and wooden shacks stretched far out across the sandy waste." By the end of the war, it was more like a modern metropolis. with macadamized roads, electric lights, miles of railway sidings, workshops, cinemas, theatres, churches, clubs, (including a fine YMCA establishment), and even a golf course. By late 1917 it had become the largest base camp in any theatre.'

A soldier of the Dorset Yeomanry described Kantara more poetically…

'There are three sounds in Egypt which never cease—the creaking of the waterwheels, the song of the frogs, and the buzz of flies. Letter writing is an impossibility in the evening, for as soon as the sun goes down, if a lamp is lighted, the air all round is thick with little grey sand-flies which bite disgustingly'.

One might imagine the soldiers of the Military Mission sweltering in the hot sun under the meagre shade of a tent, surrounded by colleagues succumbing to cholera, typhoid and malaria but they were more than likely having a 'grand old time'. Another soldier arriving at Kantara in 1917 with a fractured skull was delighted at the presence of nurses…

'It was good to see an English woman again. Had breakfast of porridge, bacon, bread and a dinner of chicken.'*

In fact, conditions at Kantara were most likely superior to the conditions granddad would encounter in Ireland over the course of his life as a Garda.

---

*The above quotes are taken from *Hell in the Holy Land* by David Woodward, personal accounts from the diaries and letters of British soldiers.

H.M.S. Izar. at Port
d at 11 am en-rout
England via Mal
Gibraltar (Spain.) &
led at 3 pm on th
e date. We arrived
Malta at 12 noon o
day 13th June 1920 &
ed again at 5 pm.
### same date. We
ted the coast of
thern Africa at 10 am
Monday 14th June 192
d not lose sight
until 11 am on Tuesd
June 1920.. At 8 am o

# Chapter Eleven: Frying Pan to Fire

## The H.M.T. Czar

The H.M.T. or S.S. Czar was a passenger ship launched in March 1912. In 1919 and 1920 she was used to transport British troops throughout 1919 and 1920 primarily from the Mediterranean to Britain but also served in the North Russian campaign. She was sold on and renamed a number of times - The *Estonia*, The *Pulaski* —while continued to ply routes between Europe and New York. She served as a troopship in WWII and was renamed The Empire Penryn in 1946 before being scrapped in 1949.

FIG. 22. THE CZAR. PHOTOGRAPHER UNKNOWN/PUBLIC DOMAIN. SOURCE WIKIPEDIA.

*"We arrived at Malta at 12 noon on Sunday 1th June 1920 & sailed again at 5pm on the same date. We sighted the coast of Northern Africa at 10am on Monday 14th of June 1920 & did not lose sight of it until 11am on Tuesday 15th June 1920. At 8am on Wed. 16th June we sighted the coast of Spain. We arrived at Gibraltar at 5pm on the same date & sailed again at 12:30 pm on Thursday 17th June 1920. We sighted the coast of Portugal at 7am on Friday 18th June 1920 and it was still in sight until 7pm on the same date."*

Of Russia, there is not a lot left to say. The adventure was over. Malta, where they had anchored in the sparkling seas under the yellow walls of Valletta, quickly receded aft along with all traces of exotic, warmer climes which had barely teased the edge of the voyage, the dark heart of which, Russia, much have seemed already like a dream, or possibly a nightmare. The next dry land my granddad's feet would walk would belong to a nation that Ireland were at war with.

## The Irish War of Independence

The War of Independence was a guerrilla war between the IRA and the British government that spanned the years from 1919 to July of 1921. The War of Independence had ignited when revolutionaries Sean Treacy, Dan Breen and Seamus Robinson assassinated two Royal Irish Constabulary (RIC) men in Solheadbeg, Tipperary, in 1919. During the last week of granddad's voyage home, the RIC, caught between their British employers and the Irish Republican Army (IRA), who were agitating for independence from the Crown, finally mutinied. RIC men, as representatives of the British government had been targets for the IRA though most were Irish. The RIC mutiny occurred after a speech from Lieutenant Colonel Bruce Smyth at Listowel on the 19th of June. Smyth announced that martial law would be introduced on June 21st, incidentally the day granddad would arrive back in Southampton. Smyth, accompanied by General Tudor, Commander of the Black and Tans - a force created by the British from ex-servicemen and deployed to Ireland in March 1920 and known, along with the later Auxiliaries, for their viciousness - declared that the RIC would be required to...

*'...wipe out Sinn Fein and any man who is not prepared to do this is a hindrance and had better leave the job immediately.'*

Constable Jeremiah Mee responded by taking off his cap and arms. Kathleen Napoli McKenna described the moment...

*'By your accent you are English and in your ignorance you forget you are addressing Irishmen. These too are English, take them and go to hell you murderer.'*

(Quoted in Tim Pat Coogan's, *Michael Colllins, Part 1*, as published by The Irish Independent, 2006, *p.165*)

Smyth ordered Mee arrested but his colleagues refused to do so. Smyth was assassinated by the IRA a month after his speech. Sean Treacy did not have long to live either. Granddad would witness his killing.

***

Granddad had been deemed discharged as of his leaving Russia in April 1920 and he probably went straight back home to Dublin that June. Until 1922 he would work the British Ordnance depot at Islandbridge Barracks, Dublin, as a stores clerk. Incidentally Mick McDonnell, one of IRA director Michael Collin's Special Squad, had a connection at Islandbridge who managed to pass him much needed arms at this time. There is no mention of a name, but I think it unlikely to have been granddad.

When Sean Treacy was killed, granddad was out walking, probably on the way from Islandbridge to his mother's house in East Wall.

He described the incident in a letter to the Irish Independent newspaper in 1967, in reply to an interview with Colonel David Neligan in that same paper.

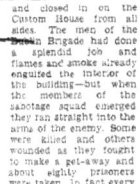

**FIG. 23. NEWSPAPER 1967. COURTESY ANTHONY SCOTT.**

*Prior to the shooting I was walking down North Earl Street towards Talbot Street when a lorry containing British troops passed by traveling slowly. I walked on into Talbot Street with the lorry only a short distance ahead of me. As the lorry reached the Republican Outfitters shop, I saw Sean Treacy - of course I did not know who he was then - running up the street in my direction with a gun in his hand. At this time the lorry was practically (if not actually) stopped and a man in mufti jumped out of it and pursued Treacy who fired a shot or two in the direction of the lorry. Both men came to grips, just as Colonel Neligan describes it, outside a pork butcher's shop and were struggling when shots were fired from the lorry, killing them both. Some of the bullets from the lorry went through the pork shop window and others went into the foyer of the adjoining Masterpiece Cinema. Obviously, as Colonel Neligan had said, the soldiers in the lorry had panicked.*

Neligan was an Irish spy for from 1916 to 1921 and deeply embedded in Dublin Castle, the seat of government and the occasion of granddad's letter was the publication of Neligan's *The Spy in the Castle*, the name by which he was known. Many would have witnessed the escalation of violence on the streets of Dublin. It was hard not to get caught up in the chaos. This was a war fought in the streets and tenements, no one really was safe. Indeed, my great-uncle on my maternal side was at Croke Park on the original Bloody Sunday when 14 spectators at a hurling match were gunned down by the British. My second cousin wrote to say ...

*'My father, William MacNamara, was in Croke Park on Bloody Sunday on 21 Nov, 1920. He was aged 18 years and was living in Dublin, probably with his brother Robert, and learning the drapery trade. Fortunately, all that he lost was his shoe as he jumped over the wall of Hill 16 to safety!!'*

William, or Bill, McNamara was brother to my granddad John MacNamara. Bloody Sunday and the killing of Sean Treacy had been in retaliation for Michael Collins Squad's assassination of a number of British agents called the Cairo Gang.

The violence was reduced somewhat between July 11th 1921, when a truce was called, and December 6th 1921 when a treaty was agreed. The Black and Tans and the Auxiliaries would begin clearing out of Ireland in January 1922. But from January to June of 1922 the tension escalated even more dramatically.

## The Treaty

The terms of the treaty had been hashed out in London between the British and the Irish delegation which included Michael Collins. This treaty saw the partitioning of the six northern counties, something Collins saw as temporary. However, some in the IRA did not agree with the terms of the Treaty and led by Eamon De Valera, or Dev, these anti-treatyites split from the Irish Republican Army or the IRA.

During this time there were four governments existing simultaneously. The British, the interim Irish Government (which would have been made up of those Irish MPS who had sat in parliament), the new Free State Government or Provisional Government (pro-treaty) and the IRA anti-treaty government. Additionally, the RIC were being disbanded to make way for a Free State Police Force which was not yet in existence. This meant policing was sparse and crime was on the rise. Much of the crime would have been connected to the war, with the IRA staging robberies of banks and post offices across the country.

The IRA split was greatly encouraged by Dev who gave inflammatory speeches against the Treaty while making a pact with Michael Collins and the New Free State. The pact and a 'rigged' election, allowed a proportional number for each party (who had to be pro-pact) to run for election in June in order to form a coalition government. As an indication that there were other things on most people's minds and how unpopular the fighting was with the majority of the Irish, there were also independent candidates that ran for other interests e.g., farming and wages. Incidentally there was a Post Office strike for higher wages in September 1922 at the height of the Civil War. Not surprisingly then the overall vote in the election was pro-treaty and for peace.

**Civil War once more**

The Civil War would kick off in Dublin city when, in April 1922 the anti-treaty IRA began to occupy pertinent buildings in the capital, making their HQ at the Four Courts, one and half miles down the Liffey from Islandbridge on my granddad's walk home. They also occupied Kilmainham Jail literally just over the road from Islandbridge and placed snipers at army barracks throughout Dublin most notably Beggars Bush Barracks. By June, events, including kidnappings and assassinations had reached a point that gave the new Free State Army no option but to attack the Four Courts. Within days the rebels had surrendered, and Dublin was back under control. So granddad would be safe on his walk home again. But only for a while. The fighting then shifted to the south and west of the country where the anti-treaty IRA dug in to conduct a guerrilla war of the kind the pro-treaty Michael Collins had excelled at. They would have to be rooted out. There was a national call to arms which granddad answered.

## Kerry

At the age of 22, granddad was on his way to the central theatre of his second civil war. Training and preparation were completed by July 27th and, assigned to The Dublin Guard in a role he referred to as Military Policeman, within the week he would be on board the *Lady Wicklow* en route to Kerry as part of a plot to sneak into anti-treaty territory by the back door. He was one of the 450 men that landed at Fenit, taking the rebels, ensconced in their southwest stronghold, by surprise. The bomb the rebels had rigged to blow up the pier in the event of such an invasion had been disarmed in the night by locals worried about their livelihood. A luck escape for, as Niall Harrington wrote in his book, *Kerry Landing*, Fenit could have been our Gallipoli. The men on the *Lady Wicklow* fired on the rebels onshore with great intensity and within a half an hour of landing had secured the foothold in Kerry. Casualties were few. They gathered to immediately march to Tralee.

**FIG. 24 & 25. GERALD SCOTT AND FRIENDS, KERRY, 1922. PHOTOGRAPHER UNKNOWN. SOURCE: ANTHONY SCOTT.**

Granddad typically had little to say of Kerry and he did not write any account. He did relate the curious episode when he came face to face with an enemy, one he had made in far off Russia. As the man in question pulled up to a checkpoint in his ass and cart, granddad recognised him as someone he had last seen in Russia, in a bar, most likely in Novorossiysk. A fight had erupted between them after which they swore to kill each other if they saw one another again. What passed between them at the checkpoint has been lost. Perhaps it illustrates how small the world really is or how one man fighting his neighbour is a story as old as time. Or perhaps it just tells us that you can never stop Irish men fighting. I would like to think there, in the midst of the sorrow and bloodshed they managed to laugh off their brawl and carried on their separate ways.

While the balance of power was decided within the first few months, the fighting continued, and granddad stayed in Kerry until the summer of 1923. While not on such a grand scale as the Russian Civil War, the Irish Civil War, fought in such a small arena, was brutal in an intimate way. Neighbour turned on neighbour, families split into factions. The IRA would kill suspected informers and lure Free State soldiers into traps, while the officers of the Dublin Guard were responsible for atrocities too, most notably the notorious Ballyseedy massacre which saw nine rebel prisoners tied to a mine which was then detonated. Similar incidents occurred at Countess Bridge and Cahirciveen. These were said to be a retaliation for Free State Army deaths at Knocknagoshel in the same savage month of March. There was widespread outrage at the time. An enquiry named the officers responsible however that inquiry was chaired by Paddy O'Daly, commander of the Free State Army and suspected of having ordering the killings in the first place. David Neligan, once Michael Collin's man in Dublin Castle and intelligence officer in Kerry, was also thought by some to be responsible. In 2008, 1923 papers naming a group called The Visiting Committee under a Commandant Delaney as being responsible for the deaths at Cahirciveen, were released. These core officers of the Dublin Guard would have been taken from IRA Squad and Dublin IRA Active Service Unit. It was only after the entrenchment of the rebels in the south that the Dublin Guard rapidly expanded by the recruitment of many more men, including granddad who signed up at the end of July 1922.

## Guardian of the Peace

In October 1923, granddad joined the Irish State's new police force, The Garda Siochana, helped by a glowing reference from pro-Treaty Senator William O'Sullivan of Killarney. O'Sullivan was one of the first members of the Irish Senate (Seanad), which sat in December 1922, alongside W.B. Yeats and Oliver St. John Gogarty. On his first posting, at Castledermot in Co. Kildare, granddad met Elizabeth Derivan who came from Castlecomer in Co. Kilkenny. They had met in a hotel in Dun Laoghaire in Dublin and married in 1925. Elizabeth came with a dowry of £500. Soon afterwards, granddad purchased a green sports car – something I only found out towards the end of researching this history. Where the car went no one knows but it was not replaced. I suppose after all the fighting he felt he deserved one. Certainly such flashiness has been non-existent in our family since.

Life afterwards never reached the same level of upheaval, but it was not uneventful. Granddad served as a Garda Sergeant for four decades including the period of the second world war and though Ireland was neutral, that had its impact too. As mentioned before there was the mine at Cullenstown and granddad would also regularly help retrieve bodies of downed airmen and sailors which would wash up on Wexford shores. Partly due to the war-torn soil from which the Gardai sprang, much of a guard's duties were to arbitrate in the community and a local sergeant would often be called to intervene in more personal issues. One time an unmarried girl of granddad's parish was found to be pregnant. The accused father was reluctant to take responsibility. Granddad sought clarification.

*'Did you know her at all?'* asked granddad

*'Only a little bit,'* answered the accused.

*'And tell me, did you go out with her?'*

*'Only a little bit'*, was the shamefaced reply.

*'And did you kiss her?'*

*'Ah shure only a little bit…'*

*'And did you put it in at all?'*

The by now predictable reply of *'only a little bit'* sealed the coward's fate.

*'It's yours so!'* declared granddad.

Granddad played the harmonica and liked to play cards both of which he may have picked up in Russia where there would have been little to do on the long freezing nights in the barracks. He was apparently a good player too. Of the harmonica anyway.

## Graiguenamanagh

He did not always keep out of trouble though, for there was an independent streak in him and he was fond of the Guinness too and these may have been part of the reason that for the early part of his career at least he and his growing family were constantly moved around. One of his postings in the early 1930s was in Graiguenamanagh in South Kilkenny. Some sixty years later, a friend bought the old Garda barracks building there. In giving me the history of the building – which once had had its roof blown off by the IRA - he told me of a Garda Superintendent who had been on a mission to capture a particularly troublesome sergeant. Having had no success at apprehending this wily guard while on duty, one night the Superintendent in desperation climbed up and into the window of the living quarters just after the guard had finished his shift, hoping to find him with the 'drop taken'. The guard, seeing a shadow coming in through the net curtains grabbed his revolver and smacked the intruder across the head with the butt of it.

At this point in the story my friend stopped and said…

*"Strangely enough the Guard had the same surname as you…"*

It was granddad. His next posting, on the border between North and South Ireland, may have been retaliation for this incident or just to put some distance between himself and the Superintendent. It wasn't his only run in with authority. Granddad often owned an english bulldog. Each successive bulldog was always called Prince. Unsentimental man that he was, he would unhesitatingly shoot two Princes on separate occasions, once when one bit a donkey which had broken into the garden and another time when one bit his daughter Mary, my aunt, who would later die from mushroom poisoning. However, when one of the Princes cornered the local Superintendent in the garden – possibly, probably, the same Superintendent from the previous story - that dog remained

FIG. 26 WITH DACHSHUND, BALDWINSTOWN.

unpunished. Later on, perhaps realising bulldogs were not a good idea, granddad would own a dachshund.

The Gardai have always been a predominantly unarmed force, but granddad always had two guns, one a .38 and one .45 - besides the .22 rifle used for rabbits - which he kept in good order all his life. My father had a close shave with a revolver of granddad's when he was ten years old. He was messing around in the barracks when he found the .38 revolver. It was not loaded but he knew where the ammunition was and how to load it. He stuck a bullet in one of the chambers but when he tried to get it out, he could not budge it. Terrified at being caught by my granddad, he desperately tried to get the bullet free. It eventually occurred to him that the only way to do so was to shoot the gun. He duly placed the muzzle against the wall and pulled the trigger. Luckily for him the revolver, as it was designed to do, skipped the full chamber, and clicked on an empty one. The bullet fell out of its own accord. Which is why I am here I am to tell you about it.

Perhaps it is an indicator of the time he grew up in that even on his deathbed, the revolvers would still be on granddad's mind. He asked my father to dismantle them and dispose of them – possibly because they had been army issue – but by this time they were long gone.

## Family

Granny and granddad went on to have eight children, seven of whom survived to adulthood. The eldest Billy (d.2018), born in Sallypark in Waterford city and, as mentioned earlier, went to Palestine in 1947 at the age of 18 and afterwards joined the British Police Force. Michael, as a Salesian Brother, went to work in Brazil as a missionary for over 30 years. He is now 'home' He has written some stories of his time in Brazil which may soon see the light of day. My Dad, born in Ballinamult in the Comeragh Mountains in Co. Waterford, emigrated to the UK. He would also join the British Army in the 1950s, spending three years in post-war Germany before marrying my Mam who he had met in Wexford. He trained as a barrister before eventually returning to Waterford. Another brother Joe, married to Selina, settled

FIG. 27. GRANDDAD AND GRANNY WITH CHILDREN, DYMPHNA, TONY, BILLY AND MICAHEL AND COLLEAGUES.

outside Wexford where they still live. Pat (d. 2001) married and settled in Kilmore Quay not far from granddad's last posting at Baldwinstown while Dymphna married and settled in Blackwater Wexford. Mercy (d.2006) married and settled in Wicklow town. Mary as mentioned before, died in Clonaslee at the age of eight.

Granddad's diary is the heart of this book but, thinking of granny, I couldn't help considering how little adventure was available to women, how truncated their lives were. But as I progressed, I realised even that is not the full story. Women were powerful in Ireland, in the fight for independence and in the Civil War. Think of Hanna Sheehy Skeffington, Helen Cousins, Constance Markiewicz – second in command at Stephen's Green during the 1916 rebellion – and Maud Gonne. Cumann na mBan was instrumental throughout Ireland during the War of Independence and women, spied, passed messages, hid rebels as well as keeping homesteads and farms going. It is true that most women's lives were benighted by constant labour, but it came as a shock to me to realise that women had perhaps more freedom in the first part of the $20^{th}$ century than in the second, when they were pushed back into a supporting role in the post-war world. It was the ultra-conservative Dev, that villain of the Civil War era, as leader of the 'new' Ireland, who would side-line all the great Irish women of the revolution. In his constitution of 1937 pledged to 'to ensure that mothers shall not be obliged by economic necessity to engage in labour to the neglect of their duties within the home. Journalist and feminist Gertrude Gaffney wrote in the Irish Independent in May1937...

*"[DeValera]had always been a reactionary where women are concerned. He dislikes and distrusts us as a sex and his aim ever since...has been to put us in what he considers our place and to keep us there".*

He succeeded. For a time.

Granny was not any sort of woman's rights activist, but she was quite a strong person in her own right. She was a tall, stern women who made excellent rhubarb and apple tarts and stuffed the odd pound note down my jumper. Like granddad, she was

**FIG. 28 GRANNY & GRANDDAD C. 1950S**

unsentimental, and not particularly maternal. She came from a well-educated background, a family of teachers, but unlike her parents and siblings, she had no interest in becoming a teacher. She never even read a book, according to my dad, and I believe she did like a spin in a sports car back in the day. But she did not shy from the relative poverty of a Garda Sergeant's life. During the late 1940s when granddad got TB (my dad remembers him being carried out of the house 'pumping blood') and spent a year in hospital, Granny would cycle her high nelly bicycle from Baldwinstown in Wexford to Wicklow town to visit him, a distance of sixty miles. Granny's life, like granddad's, was shaped by the era she was in but does not seem to have been unhappy, in fact she seems to have always been very content with her life. Granddad retired in 1962 and they moved from the familiar, comfortable barracks of Baldwinstown where my dad grew up, to a small house near the quays in Wexford town. My memories of granny come from this time.

She was the constant presence in that house while granddad, like Winston Churchill, that instigator of the 1919 Military Mission, would emerge from the bed around lunch time, boots impeccably polished, pausing for his dinner, before heading down the town, stopping off to see my other granddad to argue about Dev before proceeding onwards for a large bottle. Or two. Though he would spend many an evening in the pub - where the presence of women was not particularly welcome - he would always wake granny up when he got home to tell her all the news.

Granddad was an ordinary man not given much to introspection. He didn't speak of Russia or Kerry to either regret or glorify them. His participation in those wars came about partly because of the era he was born into, the state of turmoil of the world he grew up in but that he volunteered for both wars and then for the Gardai suggests he was not afraid to step up. When I started looking into the Civil War and Kerry, a romantic part of me wanted to find his name written somewhere or to discover he was Michael Collin's man passing arms in Islandbridge. But I don't believe he was close to any of the history makers for good or ill. Like most of us, he was not a great mover of events. He was never a partisan or a follower of the crowd. In the end I am relieved that he did not play any grand part on the world's stage, as I believe this means that his time in Russia and Kerry was unblighted by those actions that reflected badly on some as they fought their own countrymen in the bitter battle for peace.

It seems to me that he made the decision to participate on his own terms and in doing so saw some of the world and the way men behave towards each other. Afterwards, from a posting near the capital he receded into the countryside and a career that saw him playing his part in small communities where he seemed, though self-contained, happy enough. He had played his part whatever it was, taking control of what he could and leaving the rest to fate.

***

Back on board the H.MS. Czar these things lay ahead...

*"We entered the world-famous Bay of Biscay at 11 pm on the same date."*

The Bay of Biscay is famous for sinking ships. I heard a story once about man who had been wrecked in the Bay of Biscay on a dark and stormy night. Tossed about on the black surface, his life jacket pinging out his distress, he was resigned to his fate when he noticed another sailor sliding down a huge wave towards him. When he arrived in the watery trough in which our friend floundered, he said...

'Hello. Which ship are you from?'

Both apparently survived.

*"A few hours before we entered the Bay of Biscay we saw two big sharks close to the side of our ship."*

What type of shark is anyone's guess. Whale sharks, Basking Sharks, Hammerhead Sharks and even Great White Sharks are present in the Atlantic along with many smaller species. Sharks are an ominous presence. As the mighty whale, surfacing and spouting, marked granddad's passage from the known to the unknown on the voyage out, the sharks, lurking below the surface of the wild Atlantic, menacing and huge, foretold of perils ahead…

*"We arrived at Southampton at 10am on Monday 21st June 1920 & disembarked at 11am on the same date. We left Southampton on the 3:30pm train for our depot in Uxbridge and arrived at Uxbridge at 8pm on the same date. On the following day Tuesday 22nd June 1920 at 2pm we were demobilized."*

I Remain,
Yours truly,
GScott.
Late R.A.F.
Sth. Russia.

FIG. 29. GRANDDAD, SEAVIEW TERRACE, WEXFORD. 1970S. PHOTOGRAPHER ANTHONY SCOTT.

## Mutt & Jeff

There were five campaign medals that were available to those who fought in the First World War, with some being extended to include other theatres of war like Russia. One person could get a maximum of three of these medals, with a few exceptions. Pip, Squeak and Wilfred are the nicknames for the 1914 or 1914/1915 Star, The British War Medal & The Victory Medal. Everyone who received Pip would get the other two. The British War Medal (Squeak) and the Victory Medal (Pip) were what my granddad received as he had not joined until 1918. There were 6.5 million of Squeak and 5.7 million of Wilfred given out. But not everyone who received Squeak received Wilfred but most of those who received Wilfred also had Squeak. When these two were shown together they were also known as Mutt and Jeff. Pip, Squeak & Wilfred was a British cartoon strip which ran in the Daily Mirror from May 1919, only ceasing in 1956, while Mutt & Jeff was an American cartoon strip which had been published since 1907. While it is not exactly clear why the medals were named after cartoon characters it is not surprising. Humour, after all, is often the way we deal with the worst of times.

FIG. 30 GRANDDAD'S MEDALS. PHOTOS BY AND COURTESY OF JOE AND SELINA SCOTT.

## Acknowledgements

I think my family are bemused that I spent so long over this brief notebook, written perhaps as an afterthought by a man who few seemed close to. Nevertheless, they humoured me. My Mam read every blog post on the subject, posts that ran into many more words than this book and took many more deviations. Afterwards she would text me an encouraging response. My Dad printed them all out for her to read them more comfortably and also endured several 'interviews' by me and provided me with photographs, papers and anecdotes from his childhood as well as his own time in the army. My brother John Scott read through the first draft manuscript and painstakingly noted down grammatical mistakes which were legion. A better proof-reader I could not ask for. All mistakes afterwards are my own.

My aunt Selina Scott, as someone who hit it off with granddad from the get-go, offered a unique insight into a more roguish and charming character than I expected, while her husband Joe, taciturn as the youngest in a garrulous family, seemed as bemused as my dad by my interest. Selina and Joe are guardians of granddad's medals and provided the excellent photographs. Fr. Michael Scott, the youngest priest in his Dublin parish, read the first draft and corrected some of my erroneous assumptions while providing me with insight, by letter rather than email which was very welcome. He also sent me some of his writings from his years in Brazil which has set me off planning a new spate of blog posts. Una Mac on the maternal side also showed interest and provided me with the account of my great uncle's escape on Bloody Sunday.

Outside of the family, the two people to whom I owe most are CJ Hyslop and April Munday, my fellow bloggers who read and responded to every one of my posts with enthusiasm and encouragement. It was them who kept me going really and for that at least they will get a free copy of the book. You could do worse than follow them for excellent posts on photography, UK guides (CJ) and medieval history and resources (April). Traci York springs to mind too, better blogging friend is hard to find.

My thanks also goes to other writers and friends who liked, commented on and shared my posts on social media. There were a number of regulars who also kept the whole thing afloat. You know who you are…and thanks to Niall for the fez…

# Appendices

**Suggested Reading**

I had a version of this book written with a painstakingly detailed reference list and notes but took it out in the end as I felt it took up too much space for such a small tome. I have referenced some information and direct quotes and attributed the images and you will find the sources in the bibliography. I make mention here of the books and papers which I leaned on most.

I couldn't have done without Laurie Kopisto's dissertation *The British Intervention in South Russia 1918-1920*, one of the clearest and concise accounts of the time I came across – not a small thing in such a complicated history. A PDF of it can be found online. Clifford Kinvig's 2006 book, *Churchill's Crusades: The British Invasion of Russia* was also very useful and exceptionally clear and concise on the build up to the British Intervention. I am not sure why it is not more well-known. Damien Wrights's book *Churchills Secret War: British and Commonwealth Military Intervention in The Russian Civil War, 1918-20*, which was fortuitously published in the year after I started my own research, was helpful in pointing me towards primary sources. There are accounts from people who were present or biographies of those who were there. Marion Aten's *Last Train over Rostov Bridge*, written with Arthur Orrmont, and published after Aten's death, while accused of some inaccuracy and down-played by some authors - who still use it as a primary source - is a rollicking, *Boy's Own* sort of read which also manages to convey the horror of the times and I would highly recommend it. I have not read Collishaw's memoirs *The Black Flight: The Memoir of Legendary First World War Fighter Ace* (formerly *Air Command*) in full (yet) but have certainly referenced him via others. Julian Lewis's biography of Samuel 'Kink' Kinkead, *Racing Ace,* also has a chapter on South Russia which was useful in sorting out trains and dates. I don't mention Kink here who vied with Collishaw for the top flying ace but he deserves to be remembered and read about. Major Williamson's book, *Farewell to the Don* is more thoughtful and personal and I have used his words a lot – as have many others, some without crediting him. John T. Smith's *Gone to Russia to Fight* is excellent on the RAF in South Russia and indispensable for dates. General Wrangel's memoirs, *Always with Honour*, prohibitively expensive at the start of this project, are now available courtesy of an anonymous publisher via Amazon. His is a remarkably clear account of the confusion, frustration and eventual tragedy created by the leaders of the White Army and makes clear the reasons for their failure. In January 1920 he says *"By this time I was incapable of understanding anything of anybody",* the baldness of his statement conveying his despair in the face of certain loss. General Wrangel is a particular favourite of mine in case you haven't noticed. For the Irish section Niall Harrington's *Kerry Landing* which also mentions many names of regular soldiers, was illuminating as was

*The Civil War in* Kerry and *The Summer Campaign in Kerry,* both by Tom Doyle. For Irish history of that era, any of Tim Pat Coogan's books are also a good bet. I have read and skimmed tons of other books and articles most of which should be referenced here. Any omissions are accidental and will be happy to correct any in subsequent editions.

## Other Voices

One of the best things about writing this book via a blog was receiving emails from people around the world who had similar stories to tell about their ancestors escaping though Novorossiysk. Most contacted me to say how they were delighted to hear more about events which their forebears were caught up and some shared their stories and added to my knowledge. All such contacts are greatly appreciated and acknowledged where used in the text. I have listed them below along with links to any public platforms they have established to share their own research and I would urge you to seek them out.

**Alex de Fircks** was one of the first to contact me. Her grandmother Oga Woronoff and family evacuated on The Hannover. Olga wrote a memoir called *Upheaval* about that time and it can be found online. Alex has a blog at www.alexdefircks.com

**Guy Hunt** whose grandfather was a pilot flying Camels and DH9s, with 221 squadron in 1919 based out of Petrovsk and making bombing raids from Chechen Island in the Caspian Sea. Grandfather a pilot of DH9s with 221 squadron in 1919 also contacted me. I am still in awe of how much flying was going on a mere decade after the Wright Brothers flight.

**C.K.** who was researching the evacuation of two Irish bred thoroughbred horses from Novorossiysk in 1920, possibly on HMS *Iron Duke*, also contacted me. I could not help him but remain intrigued!

**Mathias Luther**'s grandfather, grandmother, father and four siblings escaped through Novorossiysk. Mathias sent me some interesting materials and images, especially grateful for the one of the Duchess Olga at Novorossiysk. Mathias blogged about South Russia in Swedish but you can Google translate it https://novorossijsk.infopr.fi

**Alan Munes** grandfather and great uncle were both part of The Dublin Guard.

**Michael Ostrogorsky** of Blue Parrot Books in Seattle had a grandfather on Wrangel's staff in the Crimea in 1920. Cavalry Captain Vassilij Ostrogorsky met and married a White Army nurse, Michael's grandmother, in early 1920. Michael has published his archives and you can find them at www.blueparrotbooks.com

**Gloris Rogulin Blake** contacted me from the U.S. to tell me that her father escaped through Novorossiysk to Constantinople.

**David Treloar**, son of George Treloar who was also one of the last out of Taganrog, also contacted me with excerpts from his father's diary, his own writing as well as images. David has done a lot of his own research over the years but has no plans to publish, though I wish he would! George Treloar's great nephew, **Henry Hudson** also got in touch.

**Alison Ward** contacted me to say her great-great uncle Malcolm Mckenzie was at Novorossiysk too. Born in Cromarty, he enlisted in 1902 and served with the Gordon Highlanders in Peshawar and Calcutta and then in France and Flanders during the Great War. She traced him to Halifax in Nova Scotia in 1920 where he arrived as seaman on *The Pretorian*. He was to have returned to the UK after that, but she can find no more trace of him. If anyone can help you can contact me via the blog below.

**I can be contacted through the blog site for this book www.southrussiadiary.wordpress.com**

# The Other Granddad

FIG 31: JOHN MAC AND FRIEND

Unlike granddad Scott, granddad Mac was not involved in any fighting either in the war of Independence or The Civil War as far as we know. I think of him as a lover to granddad Scott's fighter. Granddad Scott was not given much warmth whereas John Mac was a handsome, charming man who would give anyone the shirt off his back. He would become friends with and then fall out with granddad Scott in the 1960s over their differing views on DeValera, that villain, who was still a towering figure in Irish politics.

John Mac came from Roscrea in Tipperary where his father and two brothers carved gravestones. With no room for another brother, he ended up in Dundalk working in a hardware shop around the time granddad Scott was in Russia. It was there he met my grandmother, Mary Woods of Inniskeen – she lived in the farm next door to poet Patrick Kavanagh, a close friend of the family. He swept her off her feet and they eloped and married in Dublin on Stephen's Green and afterwards settled in Wexford. Mary died prematurely in 1939 and granddad Mac was left with seven children to attempt to look after which proved difficult. In the end two of the boys (this book is dedicated to one of them, my uncle Jim, who died in May 2021), were sent to relatives in Dublin while my mother and her sister and the next-door neighbour pitched in to help with the rest. Granddad Mac, having developed a debilitating love of the bottle, gave up drink for good in 1947 and stayed dry until his death in 1972. He is remembered in Wexford as the best farm machinery salesman of his time at the Shelbourne co-op in Campile in Co. Wexford.

**The Campile Bombing**

It was a clear bright Monday at the end of August 1940 when two German bombers made their way across the Irish sea to Carnsore point in Co, Wexford. Following the Rosslare to Waterford train line they made their way towards the little town of Campile in southeast county Wexford. One bomber diverted to Ambrosetown and attempted to bomb the viaduct, but its bombs missed their target. The second dropped four bombs on the Shelbourne co-op in rural Campile destroying the restaurant of the creamery and part of the railway line while one bomb left a crater in a nearby field. Three women were killed: Mary Ellen Kent (30), her sister Catherine Kent (26) from Terrerath, and Kathleen

Hurley (27) from Garryduff. The death toll would have been much higher if the bombers arrived even 20 minutes earlier during the lunch hour. Both bombers flew out to sea over Duncannon and Dunmore East (AP Kearns Jun 22, 1996 IT 1996). Many saw the bombers fly in, including my own father out playing in nearby Baldwinstown. His brother, Michael (or Mick), recently sent him a copy of *Ireland's Own* magazine with an a 60th anniversary account of the bomb. In the margin he has written...

*'Remember this day?! When the windows rattled in the barracks and mammy took us down the garden to shelter under the trees! I saw the 'offending' plane pass over...did you? I don't think I'm hallucinating!'*

The reasons for the bombing remain unclear but a number of theories have been floated. That the pilots mistook Wexford for England by mistake or due to British interference with the radar. The was talk that the Germans were warning the neutral Irish to maintain their neutrality (not a great argument that) or more possibly not to supply the British army with food stuffs. Granddad Mac like many others escaped being either on a day off or having had lunch and already cycling away to some farm or other.

When my parents married, my granddads became friends for a while. Granddad Scott would call in to granddad Mac on the way to the pub. My father suspects this was more to get a free read of a newspaper than any particular warmth. My granddads would eventually fall out over Eamonn De Valera. Granddad Mac was a Dev supporter while granddad Scott probably thought Dev was short for 'Devil'. Perhaps granddad Scott became heated over reading The Irish Press which, though having the advantage of being free for him to read, was controlled by the De Valera family. The granddad's different experiences informed their opinions. Granddad Mac was a romantic and probably responded to Dev's romantic view of old Ireland. Granddad Scott had experienced first-hand the fallout from the egos of great men, particularly Dev, and the cost of it to the rest of us. A free read of a newspaper could not traverse that rift.

# Select Bibliography

Alston, C., (2007), *Russia's Greatest Enemy? Harold Williams and the Russian Revolutions,* London: Tauris.

Aten (Cpt.), M. H., Orrmont, A., (1962), *Last Train Over Rostov Bridge*, London: Ashgrove Publishing.

Brady, C., (2000), 2nd ed., *Guardians of the Peace: The Irish Police*, Prendeville Publishing.

Chamberlain, W.H., (1987), *The Russian Revolution, Volume II: 1918-1921: From the Civil War to the Consolidation of Power,* New Jersey: Princeton University Press.

Colledge, J. J.; Warlow, Ben 2006. *Ships of the Royal Navy: The Complete Record of all Fighting Ships of the Royal Navy* Rev. ed. London: Chatham Publishing.

Coogan, T., P. (2006), *Michael Collins, Part 1*, Dublin: The Irish Independent.

Coogan, T., P. (2016), *The Twelve Apostles*, London: Head of Zeus.

Cording, W.J., (c.1919), *The Diary of Private W.J. Cording*. Privately published.

Duffy, J., (2015), *Children of the Rising* Dublin: Hachette, pp 175-176.

East Wall for All (2017), *World War One and the History of the North Docks*, [online] http://eastwallforall.ie

McGreevy R., (2014), *Irish soldiers in the first World War: who, where and how many?* in *The Irish Times* August 2nd.

Gunn, R., (1970), *Raymond Collishaw and The Black Flight (Air Command)*, Toronto: Dundurn Books.

Grinevetsky, S., R., et al (2014*), The Black Sea Encyclopedia*, New York: Springer Publishing.

Halpern, P., (2011), *The Mediterranean Fleet, 1919–1929*, Ashgate Publishing.

Harrington, N., (1992), *Kerry Landing*, Dublin: Anvil Books,

Kinvig, C., (2006), *Churchill's Crusade: The British Invasion of Russia 1918-1920*, New York: Hambledon/Continuum.

Kopisto, L., (2011), *The British Intervention in South Russia 1918-1920* (Academic Dissertation), Helsinki: University of Helsinki.

Lewis, J., (2013), *Racing Ace: The Fights and Flights of Samuel 'Kink' Kinkead*, Barnsley: Pen & Sword Books.

Lincoln, W. B., (1989), *Red Victory: A History of the Russian Civil War,* New York: Simon & Schuster.

Murphy, A., (2000), *The Russian Civil War: Primary Sources*, New York: Spring.

Neligan, D., (1999), *The Spy in the Castle*, Dublin: Prendeville.

Occleshaw, M., (2006), *Dances in Deep Shadows: Britain's Clandestine War in Russia 1917-1920*, London: Constable &

Paustovsky, K., (1982), *The Story of a Life*, Vol. 3: *In That Dawn.* London: Harvill Press.

Raleigh, D.J., (2002), *Experiencing Russia's Civil War*, 354-87, Princeton: Princeton University Press.

Smele, J., (2016), *The Russian Civil Wars, 1916-1926: Ten Years That Shook the World*, Oxford: Oxford University Press.

Smith, J., T., (2010), *Gone to Russia to Fight: The RAF in South Russia 1918-1920*, London: Amberley.

Tinsley, B., (2009), *The Cullenstown Strand. Tragedy*, on the Curragh History Forum, (website).

Tolstoy, A., (1991), *The Ordeal: Part II - The Year 1918*, Moscow: Raduga.

Volkov, E., V., (2014), *Volunteer Army*, in: 1914-1918, *International Encyclopedia of the First World War*, ed. by Ute Daniel et al, trans. Goldberg, G., issued by Freie Universität Berlin.

Williamson, H.N.H, (1971), *Farewell to the Don: The Journal of Brigadier H. N. H. Williamson*, London: Collins.

Woodward, David, R., (2013), *Hell in the Holy Land*, Lexington: The University of Kentucky Press.

Wrangel, Peter N., (1928), *Always with Honour: Memoirs of General Wrangel*, Robert Speller & Sons. New York. 1957 ed.

Wright, D., (2017), *Churchill's Secret War with Lenin: British & Commonwealth Intervention in the Russian Civil War*, Solihull: Helion.

Index

Aten, Marion, 102, 120, 153, 230
B Flight, 101, 102, 104, 120, 122, 145, 173
Baldwinstown, xiii, 27, 63, 216, 218
*Benbow, the*, xii, 140, 141, 143
Bingham, Lieutenant Colonel, xiii, 162
Black Army, the, 89
Black Sea, xvii, xviii, 59, 61, 66, 72, 73, 97, 141, 149, 150, 151, 160, 161, 172
Bloody Sunday, 201
Bolsheviks, xvii, 9, 39, 66, 67, 73, 75, 80, 81, 84, 87, 88, 100, 105, 106, 117, 127, 129, 137, 143, 145, 162, 164, 167, 173
Bridges, General Sir Thomas, 160
British Expeditionary Force, 10
Castlecomer, 210
Caucasus, 44, 64, 67, 72, 73, 81
Churchill, Winston, xi, xvii, 9, 10, 14, 44, 74, 75, 82, 129, 160, 168, 218
Civil War, Irish, xviii, 203, 216

Civil War, Russian, 80, 85, 86, 102, 124, 127
Clydebank, 5
Collins, Michael, 200, 201, 202, 203
Collishaw, Raymond, xii, 99, 100, 107, 108, 122
Constantinople, xi, xvii, 26, 41, 43, 44, 48, 49, 51, 52, 55, 159, 160, 163, 166, 183, 186, 187, 188, 234
Cording, William James, 19, 20, 33, 35, 189, 241
Cossacks, 72, 74, 79, 83, 84, 85, 89, 124, 128, 142, 161, 164, 165
Couche, Lieutenant H.J., 106
Cullenstown, mine, 63, 210
Dardanelles, 10, 43, 61, 188
Denikin, General Anton, 81, 105, 129, 159
De Valera, Eamon 202, 216, 218
Dervishes, xviii, 53, 55
Dublin, xvii, xviii, 6, 7, 8, 12, 26, 97, 150, 198, 200, 203, 207, 209, 210, 227
Dublin Guard, 207, 209, 212, 234

245

East Wall, 6, 150, 198
Ekaterinodar, 78, 94, 129, 145, 160
Emperor of India, the, 143, 174
France, xvii, 12, 13, 14, 17, 48, 188
Frecheville, Captain William, xii, 106
Free State, xviii, 8, 202, 203
Garda Siochana, 63
George, Lloyd 10, 75, 188
Glasgow, 5
*Gone to Russia to Fight*, 99, 123, 127, 129, 153
Great War, the, 84
Green Guards, the (Green Army) 88, 130, 136, 137, 138, 140, 142, 143, 149, 152, 164, 167
*Hannover*, the, xiii, 173, 175, 184, 233
Harrington, Niall, 207
Holman, General Herbert, xii, 77, 78, 79, 87, 108, 109, 121, 129, 147, 159, 160, 164, 183
IRA, 8, 197, 198, 202, 203, 212
Islandbridge Barracks, 198
Kerry, xi, xiii, xviii, 207, 209, 219
Kerry Landings, xviii, 207

Kolchak, General, 74, 80, 81
Kopisto, Lauri, 105, 106, 138
Kornilov, General, 81
Last Train Over Rostov Bridge, 153
Lemnos, 37, 38
Loch Lomond, 5
Lock Out, xviii
Makhno, Nestor, xii, 72, 89
Malta, xvii, xviii, 26, 31, 33, 35, 36, 37, 196
Mamontov, General, 128
Maund, Lieutenant Colonel Arthur, 99, 121
Mosque St. Sophie, 44, 46, 47
Moudross, 37, 38
Mount Etna, xviii, 29
Napoleon, 26
Neligan, Colonel David, 199, 200
*Novorossisk*, xii, xiii, xvii, xx, 65, 66, 67, 72, 73, 74, 75, 78, 79, 94, 104, 105, 115, 117, 122, 130, 133, 136, 137, 138, 140, 142, 143, 144, 145, 146, 147, 149, 150, 152, 153, 154, 159, 160, 162, 163, 165, 166, 167, 168, 172, 174, 183, 184, 233, 234
Novorossiysk, xx, 66, 79, 115, 130, 138, 140, 145,

146, 153, 154, 160, 162, 168, 234, 235
Orel, 74, 84, 104
Paustovsky, Konstantin, 178
plague, xviii, 49, 186
quarantine, xviii, 183, 186
RAF, 12, 78, 99, 101, 103, 104, 107, 121, 122, 172
Railway, 94
Red Army, 87, 137
Red Terror, the, 127
RIC, 197, 202
Rising, the, xviii, 7
Rostov, xiv, 72, 85, 94, 104, 105, 106, 107, 117, 120, 122, 123, 124, 125, 127, 128, 145, 173
Russian Imperial Navy, 39
Scott, Anthony, xiii
Scott, Elizabeth, xiii, 227,
Scott, Kathleen, xiv
Scott, William, 5, 7
Second World War, xix, 14
Smith, John T., 99, 123, 127, 153
Sopwith Camels, 101, 109, 172
South Russia, xiv, xvii, xviii, 10, 55, 62, 69, 74, 75, 77, 80, 94, 99, 163, 234
Taganrog, xvii, 72, 74, 78, 79, 94, 97, 99, 100, 103, 104, 105, 107, 115, 116, 117, 120, 121, 123, 124, 144, 153, 159, 234
Treacy, Sean, xviii, 198, 200, 201
Treloar, Major George, 122
Trotsky, Leon, 66
Tsarists, 10, 72, 73
Volunteer Army, 10, 79, 80, 81, 82, 129, 166
Waterford, xvii, 26, 215
Wexford, xiii, 27, 63, 150, 211, 215, 218
White Army, xvii, xx, 10, 55, 66, 67, 73, 74, 75, 79, 80, 85, 86, 94, 99, 102, 104, 106, 116, 128, 129, 137, 149, 154, 159, 161, 234
Williamson, Major H.N.H, 127, 128, 146, 147, 153, 161, 164, 166, 167, 231, 243
Wrangel, General Pytor, xii, 82, 84, 85, 86, 102, 116, 121, 142, 154, 160, 166, 234
Wright, Damien, 105, 129, 168, 171, 178

www.southrussiadiary.wordpress.com

www.ingramcontent.com/pod-product-compliance
Lightning Source LLC
Chambersburg PA
CBHW040108120526
44589CB00040B/2803